Praise for *Luminous*

"*Luminous* is the kind of book that is a pleasure to recommend to others. David Beck writes with the head of a scholar and the heart of a pastor, giving us a book that is full of wisdom made extremely practical. This is a great guide for any who care about living their faith, not just talking about it."
Tim Morey, pastor at Life Covenant Church and author of *Embodying Our Faith*

"David Beck's book is luminous. He uses 'luminous' to indicate that Christians are called to reflect Jesus' shalom in and through our lives. I'm using 'luminous' to describe the content of his book, which is clear, glowing and lovely in every way. Beck incorporates Scriptures and stories to illustrate his points, and his creative and practical suggestions are easy to try. His book is a luminous invitation to go deeper into the life of faith, to love and serve Jesus more deeply so we can shine."
Lynne M. Baab, author of *Sabbath Keeping*

"Suggests the dangerously bright possibility that we can be tuned into and turned on by the same light that illuminates the whole universe with the love of God. We should pay attention to Beck, because he writes from lived knowledge of practicing the presence of God amidst the messy details of life."
Mark Scandrette, author of *Practicing the Way of Jesus* and *Free*

"Rooted in the incarnation and our missionary God, *Luminous* offers both an inspiring vision of what living with Jesus and surrendering to his purposes truly looks like, as well as practical steps to carry it out. Surrender and shine!"
Tom Lin, vice president, InterVarsity Christian Fellowship

"This book is a remarkable achievement. Written with charm and simplicity, it provides a point of entry into the spiritual life that is refreshing and engaging. Beck draws deeply on the core of the Christian faith in the work of the Son and the Spirit in a way that is honest and salutary. His feet are firmly planted on the ground; his mind is saturated with the life and Spirit of Christ; and his heart radiates a realistic love. Through it all he draws us gently but firmly into a new world of grace and action."
William J. Abraham, Perkins School of Theology, Southern Methodist University

LIVING THE PRESENCE

LUMINOUS

AND POWER OF JESUS

T. DAVID BECK

IVP Books

An imprint of InterVarsity Press
Downers Grove, Illinois

InterVarsity Press
P.O. Box 1400, Downers Grove, IL 60515-1426
World Wide Web: www.ivpress.com
Email: email@ivpress.com

InterVarsity Press® *is the book-publishing division of InterVarsity Christian Fellowship/USA*®, *a movement of students and faculty active on campus at hundreds of universities, colleges and schools of nursing in the United States of America, and a member movement of the International Fellowship of Evangelical Students. For information about local and regional activities, write Public Relations Dept., InterVarsity Christian Fellowship/USA, 6400 Schroeder Rd., P.O. Box 7895, Madison, WI 53707-7895, or visit the IVCF website at www.intervarsity.org.*

All Scripture quotations, unless otherwise indicated, are taken from THE HOLY BIBLE, NEW INTERNATIONAL VERSION®, *NIV*® *Copyright* © *1973, 1978, 1984, 2011 by Biblica, Inc.*™ *Used by permission. All rights reserved worldwide.*

While all stories in this book are true, some names and identifying information in this book have been changed to protect the privacy of the individuals involved.

Cover design: Cindy Kiple
Interior design: Beth Hagenberg

ISBN 978-0-8308-3580-5 (print)
ISBN 978-0-8308-6471-3 (digital)

Printed in the United States of America ∞

Library of Congress Cataloging-in-Publication Data
A catalog record for this book is available from the Library of Congress.

P	18	17	16	15	14	13	12	11	10	9	8	7	6	5	4	3	2	1
Y	28	27	26	25	42	23	22	21	20	19	18	17	16	15	14	13		

To Susan

CONTENTS

INTRODUCTION

Moving to the Center

I TRUDGED UP THE INCLINE of a rock-strewn dirt road in Port-au-Prince with nine-year-old Lizyanna riding on my back and her sister and two brothers walking alongside. Lizyanna was running a high fever, and I was carrying her home to the makeshift shelter where her family was temporarily staying. She was quiet while I chatted with the other kids in the best Creole I could manage. Nearly everywhere we looked there were broken walls or collapsed houses, reminding us of the earthquake that had devastated Haiti a month before. I was midway through a thirty-two-day stay at the Maison de Lumiere orphanage. It proved to be a life-changing trip that shifted my conception of what it means to be a Christian.

Earlier that afternoon, I had been playing with Lizyanna at Maison de Lumiere's feeding program. Lizyanna had been darting around as she usually does. For a few minutes I had played chase with her. Lizyanna is an incredibly fast runner, and I have yet to catch her when we play chase. I had no idea she was ill until after she ate. As the other kids got up and ran off, Lizyanna slumped at the table, looking listless. I walked over to her and asked, *"Ou malad?"* (Are you sick?). Not even lifting her eyes, she slowly nodded. I told her I would get her sister and brothers and we would walk to the orphanage's medical clinic, a few houses away. There the nurses gave Lizyanna a dose of Tylenol, and we discussed further care.

I decided to accompany the kids home, so we set out from the clinic to the tent they were living in—a walk of about four city blocks. Lizyanna was weak, and I offered to carry her. She has striking features but is hardy and wiry, being raised street-tough in dire poverty. Running around with a fever is not unusual for a kid like her. Still, when I offered to carry her home, her face visibly softened, and she readily accepted. It was an unusual display of vulnerability.

As I carried her along, Lizyanna wrapped her arms around my shoulders and laid her head on my back. Soon I noticed that she was slumping and starting to slide down my back. I turned my head and asked her, *"Ou okay?"* In a barely audible voice, she half-whispered, *"M' malad"* (I'm sick). I hoisted her higher, she wrapped her arms around my neck, and we continued walking. A couple of minutes later she slumped again, we whispered back and forth, and I hoisted her up my back. We would repeat this sequence several times between the medical clinic and her house. It moved me to see her so weak.

In those few minutes the rest of the world seemed to fade away, and I felt connected—to Lizyanna on my back, to her brothers and sister walking beside me, to the rocky and dusty road, to the heat of the sun, to the smells of Haiti, and to the sense that I was participating in a vibrant compassion much greater than myself. I was being given the chance to express God's love in a very simple and down-to-earth way to my remarkably tough but suddenly frail little friend. I felt like I was walking on holy ground.

I recalled a picture that had formed in my mind as others prayed over me before I had left for Haiti. Such pictures are a rare occurrence for me, and in fact, I can still see the image in my mind today. I saw a street in gray-scale tones. On both sides, buildings were broken, and rubble had spilled into the street. It represented postearthquake Haiti. Walking away from me down the middle of the street was a robed figure I knew to be Jesus. He was in the midst of that broken city, walking the streets and ministering to the dying, hurt and grieving.

I was awed by Jesus' compassion but surprised by what came next. I was in the wrong place. I wasn't supposed to applaud Jesus from the edge of the picture. I was to be in the center of it—right where Jesus was. He wanted to be present in those streets *through me*. The idea was exciting but daunting. I couldn't figure out how to do something like that. Plus it felt wrong—almost irreverent— to think of walking over and standing where Jesus was. Something in me wanted to keep a respectful distance from him. Puzzled, I had filed the picture away in my mind.

Now, in the middle of a Haitian road, this picture came back to me, and I was thunderstruck that it was being fulfilled. It was as if God was whispering, "You remember what I showed you? You're doing it right now." I hadn't thought about it or planned it. I had simply responded to someone's need in the Spirit of Jesus. The spontaneity of the situation and a prayerful attitude helped me be an open vessel for Jesus' love. I found myself in the center of a stunning picture God was rendering—an enactment of Jesus' raw, simple and concrete love.

Although a lot of good things happened as I fulfilled my official duties during that trip, God chose the unspectacular deed of taking four children home to produce a powerful awakening in me. In those few minutes with Lizyanna and her siblings on that dirt road, more than thirty years of following Jesus, eight years of full-time theological study and almost a decade of vocational ministry were suddenly, and surprisingly, distilled down to their essence: the calling to be a carrier of Jesus' presence and a vessel of his love. This book arose from the desire to be in the center of Jesus-pictures not just on special trips but in the everyday world.

STAYING ON THE EDGE OF THE PICTURE

As I gained clarity about the Christian life on that dirt road, other insights soon fell into place. I was able to see why over the preceding years I had been growing increasingly frustrated with my spiritual life. I had often been settling for the edges of the picture. I knew a lot *about* Jesus and did things *for* him, yet I wasn't always *with* him. He wanted to close the distance between us. Moreover, I observed that a lot of other Christians are wilting because they live with the same kind of distance between themselves and Jesus. In our culture, there are two popular approaches to being a Christian that perpetuate the problem. I have tried them both extensively. They are centered in knowing and doing.

Knowing. This approach sounds convincing: we become most effective as Christians when we build up our knowledge of God, shape our thought life according to the Scriptures, and let truth dictate how we behave. These are all good aspirations. But alarmingly, I have noticed that seeking knowledge can actually become a way to hide from God. Never has there been a society that serves up so much information about God, and it is easy for us to become so enamored with sacred information that we rarely deal with what is going on in our hearts. I personally have felt distance grow in my relationship with God when I have slipped into substituting learning about him for communing with him. I long for connection with God and his world in ways that theological study alone can't deliver.

I have found out for myself what the spiritual masters in the Christian tradition have been talking about for centuries: knowing God in our heads leaves us wanting to know him deeper in our hearts.

Doing. Another popular approach to the Christian life revolves around doing. We follow Jesus by doing some deeds he did or might do. We work to see results in our lives and the world around us—and if we don't see results quickly enough, we search for a more effective approach. Like knowledge, performance is admirable and necessary. I certainly want to see God transform us and the world, and there is never a time when imitation of Jesus isn't important. Paul said, "Follow my example, as I follow the example of Christ" (1 Cor 11:1). However, we run into problems when the question that defines our relationship with God is "What would Jesus *do*?" Just like knowing, doing can become a place where we hide from God. When we focus on our actions and their results, we grow estranged from God. Our desire to be productive *for* Jesus can block our availability to be present *with* Jesus in a broken and needy world.

Perhaps you are a Christian and have spent lots of energy on knowing and doing, only to find that you are dissatisfied with the distance between you and Jesus. Or perhaps you are not a Christian, and you want to know whether there is anything in the Christian life that you can't get from reading about Jesus and being compassionate. This book is meant to guide you toward the sweet spot of joining Jesus in a union beyond understanding, where he shines vibrantly through you.

THE DIFFERENCE BETWEEN LIVING FOR JESUS AND LIVING WITH JESUS

There is a vast difference between living *for* Jesus by knowing and doing religious things, and living *with* Jesus by walking each day in his presence. Living *for* Jesus might start out looking great, but it eventually leads to a lifeless existence of going through the Christian motions. We can go to church, be nice, read the Bible, pray, give money and create a safe home—and over time grow tired and passionless. For practicing Christians, this is an alarmingly common trap.

I know well the hollowness of this life. Even after that trip to Haiti and its clarifying experience, like an addict I have found myself relapsing into going through the motions for Jesus. The more hectic life gets, the more I want to gobble up information for solving my most urgent problems and hunker down with my to-do list. Jesus recedes into the background. I like to think I have staked everything on my relationship with Jesus, so when I realize that I have relapsed, I'm flooded with all sorts of distressing thoughts. *Maybe I shouldn't be a pastor* is one of those three-o'clock-in-the-morning topics. And yet I feel that experiencing this struggle is exactly one of the reasons God called me to be a pastor.

Living *with* Jesus is a completely different experience. It is an intensely personal encounter with God, whoever is in front of me, and whatever is happening. It is open-hearted and multi-sensory. It is being right here, in this moment. It is a radical alternative to our growing social norm of being so saturated in multitasking that we can pay only "continuous partial attention"[1] to God or people.

We are returning to the thoroughly relational heart of the Christian faith. We are pulling Jesus' Great Commandments to love God and people off the shelf of memorable teachings and implementing them as a moment-to-moment way of life. There is nothing richer. When we live with Jesus, we find his words to be true: "I have come that they may have life, and have it to the full" (Jn 10:10).

As we live with Jesus, we find that our relationships with people become transformed. This includes both "who" and "how." Instead of controlling our social lives or settling into comfortable circles that only reinforce the status quo, we open ourselves to let God connect us with whomever he chooses—people of other religions or political views, people who wear us out, people who make us laugh, people who encourage us and so on. Not only do we allow God to choose our social circles for us, we also allow him to determine how we interact with those people. Instead of manipulating people and situations to get what we want, we say and do what is needed to build others up and draw them closer to God.

Living with Jesus includes not only the way we relate to God and one another. It also gives us a common cause in this world. We become people who are gazing and reaching toward a single horizon. We become agents of God's *shalom*—the state in which all is made well in the world—God has everything just the way he wants it. Shalom means justice, peace, abundance and harmony. There is no greater life-purpose than to join together in ushering in this new reality. Jesus is the Prince of Shalom. To shine is to be a shalom-maker. Shalom-makers look like ordinary people who are willing to do extraordinary things to see broken, downtrodden and oppressed people set free to thrive in this world.

Living with Jesus is not just about us gaining a new experience of the Christian life. It includes something that happens *in* us, but it is a lot more than that. It is also something that happens *through* us. Let's return to that dirt road in Port-au-Prince. The key wasn't that I was focused on acquiring a new level of self-awareness or fulfillment—although that certainly was a powerful experience. Rather, more radically than is normal for me, I was tuned in to Jesus and the people I was serving. Everything I had to offer—physical strength, relationship with God, theological training, sense of humor, compassion, broken Creole—was in use, but in an other-focused way. I was aware of what I was thinking, doing and feeling, but it was emphatically and refreshingly not about me. In that other-focused engagement I found the presence of God.

JESUS SHINES THROUGH THOSE WHO LIVE WITH HIM

To live with Jesus is to dwell in his presence, love others and make shalom. As we follow him by obeying his leadings and taking on his character, he performs a miracle. He shines his own divine light through us. We come to fulfill Jesus' words that we are the light of the world and are here to let our light shine so others will glorify God (Mt 5:14-16). God intends for his children to be luminous.

Throughout this book I will use the image of *shining* to talk about living with Jesus. As I will explain more fully in the next chapter, brilliant light is a symbol of God's presence among us, his power to overcome whatever or whomever harms us, and his peace that comes when all is made right. In Psalms 31, 80 and 94, "Shine!" becomes a prayer, as God's people cry out to him to save them from strong enemies. In Paul's letters, "shine" is a way of summing up how Christians are to dwell in the world. It is a call to display God's presence, love others and do God's will. *To shine is to bear the shalom-making presence of Jesus in the everyday world.*

We are to shine like stars in the sky, but shining is completely down to earth. It is simple, self-forgetful, connected and practical. Shining can happen not just on a trip to a faraway country but every day of our lives. Jesus is present, and when we move with him, he shines through us to light up his world. I have found that shining happens whenever I become genuinely interested in someone else's life and well-being and prayerfully available for whatever

God wants to do in the moment. It is a pattern—when I approach people that way, I frequently experience Jesus' shining presence. *The brightness of the light that shines through us corresponds to our self-forgetfulness and personal attention to the Spirit of God and the person in front of us.* This book is an invitation to grow in Jesus' way of relational engagement so we experience the Christian life and shine with the Spirit of Christ ever more vibrantly.

GROWING IN JESUS' WAY OF SHINING

There are surely many routes that lead to spiritual growth. One of the primary aspects of my route has been internalizing a key story about God—the one story that above all others epitomizes God's shining in our world. It is the incarnation, which is the story that, *in the person of Jesus, God became human and walked among us.* Nothing says "God is relationally engaged with human beings" like God's becoming a human being himself so he could save us (see 1 Jn 4:7-12). In the person of Jesus, God left behind perfect bliss and personally and physically entered into the wonder and the grit of human existence. God clothed himself in human skin, and he walked dusty roads and ministered to the sick. He did it for a clear purpose: he wanted to unite us with himself. He embraced all of who we are so that we can embrace all of who he is.

God's becoming one of us is an exciting story, but I didn't just wake up one morning and find myself brimming with inspiration because of it. For years it had functioned for me like a theological plumb line. Like many Christians, I used it to judge the orthodoxy of others' theology. And since I wasn't judging people's orthodoxy all that often, the doctrine gathered dust. That began to change when it hit me that Christmas is a season built around the incarnation story. I reopened the incarnation—studying it, praying over it, reflecting on it and discovering all sorts of ways to practice it. Now I am like an incarnation junkie. I can't get enough of it, because it shows God right in the center of the picture of human existence and opens an invitation for us to join him there.

A LIFE OF PURPOSE, PRESENCE, POWER AND PEACE

This book is for anyone who wants to live with Jesus and shine with his light. Over my years of meditating on the incarnation narrative, certain themes have risen to the surface and become prominent. My hope and prayer for every reader is that you experience the thrill of the incarnation story, open yourself more fully to God and his world, see how he is already working through you in his way of relational engagement, and stoke within yourself a hunger for the vibrant life Jesus intends you to have.

We begin with an exploration of the biblical image of shining in chapter one. The rest of the book follows four key themes that together form an arc for practicing the incarnation story and shining with Jesus' light.

Purpose. As the incarnate Son, Jesus was in our world for a specific purpose. In chapter two we will explore the difference it makes when we join in Jesus' purpose. Very simply, you and I are on a mission—Jesus' own mission, in fact.

Presence. Nothing says "God is present" like God's becoming one of us. But we need a lot of help being present. We are plagued by a frenetic pace of life that renders us partially absent most of the time. Drawing on the story of the incarnation, chapters three through five will focus on presence from three different angles: being present with God, present in our physical bodies and present to the people around us.

Power. There is a paradox of power that arises from the incarnation narrative. Although Jesus was God-become-human, his power came out of his self-emptying and humility. Chapters six through eight lead us along Jesus' incarnational path of emptying ourselves, humbling ourselves and receiving the infilling of the powerful Spirit of God.

Peace. Being clear about our mission, living a life of presence and receiving God's power all prepare us to take action. Chapter nine fills out a picture of what that action looks like. The incarnation story shows God becoming one of us so he could build a state of shalom, where people are healed, saved and given new life, and the world ultimately comes into a state of harmony. We become shalom-makers by involving ourselves in God's ongoing compassion, mercy and justice.

A journey awaits us. A path is open in front of us. If we let Jesus live through us in everyday moments, then we will become people who shine with the presence of Jesus and change the world around us. It is possible. More than that, it is our calling. Paul prays for the Ephesians that they be filled with God's love "to the measure of all the fullness of God" (Eph 3:19). Stop and think about that for a moment. You and I, filled to the measure of *all the fullness of God.* As lofty as it is, that is our calling in Christ! We are not called just to imitate Jesus but to be carriers of his very presence.

SHINING LIKE STARS

Then you will shine among them like stars in the sky
as you hold firmly to the word of life.

PHILIPPIANS 2:15-16

I F EVER THERE WAS A PERSON who could have gotten caught up living *for* Jesus, it was Mother Teresa. The demands of ministering to people in a slum can keep one going every waking moment, leaving no time or energy to tend to one's connection to God. Mother Teresa set up shop in one of the most destitute slums in Calcutta, India. She was surrounded by people dressed in rags and suffering from hunger and disease. Children were without education. Oppression and death were commonplace. The needs were crushing and endless, and Mother Teresa was a heroine of compassion for the poorest of the poor. What has caught my attention is her spiritual life and her understanding of her calling. She could have served the poorest of the poor *for* Jesus. Instead, she served them *with* Jesus. She was a presence-bearer and an icon of shining.

Long before she began work in Calcutta, Mother Teresa per-

ceived that Jesus was sending her to be a carrier of his love into
the worst slums. As she wrestled with her call, she sensed the
persistent voice of Jesus speaking in her heart: "Come, come,
carry Me into the holes of the poor. Come, be My light."[1] Mother
Teresa wasn't out to fulfill a social agenda. She was surrendering
all in order to be a bearer of Jesus' presence where he sent her.
Her social work was astounding, but she shows us that social
justice must be placed within the context of carrying Jesus'
presence, not the other way around.

In light of her calling to be a presence-bearer, the effect Mother
Teresa had on people is worthy of note. In 1971, British television
journalist Malcolm Muggeridge wrote a book about Mother Teresa
titled *Something Beautiful for God.* Muggeridge was a hardened
religious cynic. He had been driven away from the church after
witnessing too much controversy, bickering and political maneu-
vering. Much to his surprise, he underwent a life-changing encounter with God through being around Mother Teresa. He describes her as a luminous person who shone with a transcendent
presence. "Something of God's universal love has rubbed off on
Mother Teresa, giving her homely features a noticeable luminosity;
a shining quality."[2] She was not a sophisticated theologian. She was
not rich. She was not otherwise particularly impressive. But there
was something about her that Muggeridge found irresistible and
captivating. Thousands of others had the same experience of her.
There are tales of people weeping after spending no more than a
couple of minutes with her.

Muggeridge was not a trained theologian, but he captured a
point that is central to this book. As he spent time with Mother
Teresa, the incarnation story came to echo repeatedly in his
mind. He found himself meditating on John 1:14, "The Word
became flesh and made his dwelling among us." Muggeridge

came to see this verse as a key to the Christian life. We are to live in such a way that we radiate Christ's presence. He wrote, "The Christian story is simply an endless presentation of this process of the Word becoming flesh and dwelling gracefully and truthfully among us."[3] Mother Teresa was but one example of the general truth that *the incarnation is a story that began with Jesus but continues with us.*

ORDINARY PEOPLE WHO SHINE

Lest we think that shining with the presence of Jesus is only for the Mother Teresas of the world, I have been around other people who shine like this. I think of my friend Joan. Joan is petite, and now that she is "along in years," as she would put it, she wears thick glasses. Behind those glasses are eyes that are bright with all the youthfulness of a lover of God who keeps discovering more of who he is and can't wait to share him with others. Many lives have been turned toward God because of her. Joan is British, and I have claimed her as my "adopted mum." There is something about Joan. Whenever she is around, I experience a wave of God's love and peace. Joan shines with the presence of Jesus.

And there are others. I think of my late friend David. He and I worked together as staff pastors. When I was new to vocational pastoral ministry, he took me under his wing. I was fascinated with the way people gravitated to him. He didn't preach on Sundays. He didn't do a lot of platform teaching. He wasn't a high-profile kind of pastor. But he was magnetic. When we were with him, we experienced God's love, and we couldn't get enough. After David passed away from a sudden stroke, hundreds attended his funeral. Though he was gone from us, the atmosphere in the room was drenched in God's love. Even in death, Jesus shone through David.

If Mother Teresa seems too far above the rest of us, let me assure you that my friends Joan and David are just like you and me. The point isn't how special they are but how special God is. He is the one who fills us with his presence, and it is his presence that is radiant. The question is how much we will let him shine through us. He certainly desires to. He longs for us to experience the joy and peace of deep connection with him. He is eager to reveal himself through us to a lost and confused world. He longs to transform lives through us just as he has through others who have come to radiate the presence of Jesus. He intends to continue the story of the incarnation in you and me.

GOD'S PRESENCE, POWER AND PEACE

If you were one of the disciples, how would you go about describing Jesus to people who had never seen him? You had lived with him for three-and-a-half years. His presence among people was altogether unique. You felt a bond with him that drew you forward but mystified you at the same time. You had seen him perform miracle after miracle. He healed every day of the week, even on the Sabbath. He taught with a style and authority all his own, and when he talked about God, your heart burned within your chest. His compassionate love for people was unorthodox and life-changing. You had seen even the worst characters turn toward God after having one conversation with Jesus. No one owned him, although many tried. Even when he was crucified, he went to the cross of his own accord. How in the world would you ever convey who this most remarkable Jesus was?

Here is how the disciple John did it: "In him was life, and that life was the light of all humankind. The light shines in the darkness, and the darkness has not overcome it. . . . The true light that gives light to everyone was coming into the world" (Jn 1:4-5, 9).

In the same way a picture is worth a thousand words, a good image can go a long way toward capturing the essence of a person. In John's case, he latched onto an image used in the Scriptures to talk about God bursting forth in the world to do his will. John described Jesus as the shining light.

When we look at how "shine" is used in the Scriptures, three meanings are prominent. These meanings form overarching themes in this book: presence, power and peace. First, "shine" portrays God's *presence*. Psalm 50:2 celebrates Jerusalem as the place God abides and the location from which "God shines forth." The Bible closes with John's vision of the New Jerusalem, a place in which there is no need for the sun or moon to shine because "the glory of God gives it light, and the Lamb is its lamp. The nations will walk by its light, and the kings of the earth will bring their splendor into it" (Rev 21:23-24).

Second, shining light is a way to speak of God's *power*, as when the word *shine* is used in the Psalms as a prayer for God to exercise his might. *Shine* is especially prominent in Psalm 80. The prayer opens with these words:

> Hear us, Shepherd of Israel,
> you who lead Joseph like a flock.
> You who sit enthroned between the cherubim,
> shine forth. . . .
> Awaken your might;
> come and save us. (Ps 80:1-2)

Continuing his prayer in Psalm 80, Asaph repeats the same refrain three times:

> Restore us, O God;
> make your face shine on us,
> that we may be saved. (Ps 80:3, 7, 19)

In other psalms as well, shine is an impassioned word on the lips of people crying out to God.

> The LORD is a God who avenges.
>   O God who avenges, shine forth. (Ps 94:1)

> My times are in your hands;
>   deliver me from the hand of my enemies,
>   from those who pursue me.
> Let your face shine on your servant;
>   save me in your unfailing love. (Ps 31:15-16)

God shines in many ways, from a grand display of his power like the plagues and exodus from Egypt down to small-scale miracles like individual people coming to surrender their lives to Jesus. Next time you are at church, you can look around the room and see how God has already shone among the people with whom you worship.

Third, when God shines forth in presence and power, he brings about his *peace*. Peace is what God intends to do. It is his purpose behind the use of his power. This means righting every wrong, reconciling every relationship and healing every wound. When God shines, he brings people into harmony with him and one another, and he renews creation. In other words, salvation happens. God establishes his peace, which is known in Hebrew as *shalom*.

God's light is not merely decorative. It is not here to make us look good or gain recognition. It victoriously liberates us from our enemies. Because the world is dark, God's light comes through struggle. Praying "O God, shine forth" is another way of praying, "Let your kingdom come, your will be done." In other words, we ask God to make everything the way he wants it. And when things are the way God wants them, they shine with his glory.

In my decades of being a spiritual leader, I have prayed with hundreds of people for God to save someone, repair a marriage, help someone overcome addiction, provide a job, supply food for the hungry, and address all sorts of other issues big and small. It isn't normal for us to call on God to "shine." And yet that word shows up in the Bible's prayer book, the Psalms, not once but multiple times. I suggest we allow the word "shine" to enter our prayer vocabulary. After all, when God's light shines, things happen.

Are you ready to try this on? I invite you to pause and pray for God to "shine forth" in your life and in the lives of other people. In doing so, you are expressing faith that God is present, and you are calling on him to exercise his power to bring about his peace. Only remember, when God shines, things happen. Close by verbalizing how you look forward to seeing what he will do next, and express your willingness to take part in it.

JESUS SHINES

These three themes of God's presence, power and peace converge in the person of Jesus. At Christmastime we like to quote two passages from Isaiah that looked forward to the day the Savior would come and the presence of God would break into the world in a whole new way: "The people walking in darkness have seen a great light; on those living in the land of deep darkness a light has dawned" (Is 9:2), and "Arise, shine, for your light has come, and the glory of the LORD rises upon you" (Is 60:1). The Messiah would bring with him the glory of the Lord, which is a manifestation of God's presence, power and peace. The Messiah would be the Savior, the only One mighty enough to deliver God's people from all their enemies.

Jesus shone through countless actions, but one story stands above the others to get the point across. It was as if God wanted to say, "Jesus is *the* shining light. Pay attention!" One day Jesus took Peter, James and John to the top of a mountain. As he stood there before them, suddenly he was transfigured: his face shone like the sun and his clothes became as blindingly brilliant as a flash of lightning (Mt 17:2; Mk 9:3; Lk 9:29). Whereas Moses' face had temporarily glowed after he spent forty days in God's presence on the top of Mount Sinai, Jesus' whole being shone forth in a statement that he himself was the light of God. When we think about a life of shining, we will always be pointed back to the One who shone before people with a blinding light: Jesus.

Given that "shine" is used in the Scriptures to convey the awesome realities of God's presence, power and peace, it astounds me that "shine" would be applied to us. God's light isn't only for himself. He shares it with his people. Jesus said, "I am the light of the world. Whoever follows me will never walk in darkness, but will have the light of life" (Jn 8:12). In other words, when we follow Jesus, we will gleam in a broken and dreary world. Jesus also told all his followers in the Sermon on the Mount, "You are the light of the world. . . . Let your light shine before others, that they may see your good deeds and glorify your Father in heaven" (Mt 5:14, 16).

Jesus' followers got the picture. The apostle John wrote that God is light and we are to walk in the light (1 Jn 1:5-7). Paul exhorted his readers, "For you were once darkness, but now you are light in the Lord. Live as children of light (for the fruit of the light consists in all goodness, righteousness and truth)" (Eph 5:8-9). This thought is continued in Philippians 2:12-16. Paul encourages his readers to stand out brilliantly against the darkness of their surrounding culture. "Then you will shine among them like stars in the sky."[4] We are called to give off light—not our light but the light of Jesus himself.

Being a Christian isn't about being nice churchgoers. It is about carrying the presence of Jesus everywhere we go and participating in his power to bring about shalom. It is about being a luminous person.

A PERSON OF CONTRAST

Jesus was what I call a "person of contrast." He stood out in a crowd. We are to be transformed more and more into people who shine against a dark backdrop. In the introduction, I cautioned that we too easily settle into a pattern of living *for* Jesus by relying on what we know or do, to the point that we lose a deep connection with God. Now I want to revisit knowledge and action and place them within their context. The truth is, if we want to grow spiritually and make a difference in the world, what we know and what we do are critically important. This book is an invitation to embrace knowledge and action but to set them within our calling to shine with the presence of Jesus. As we do, we will be people who see the light, follow the light and shine with the light.

See the light. To see the light is to gain knowledge about Jesus. Knowledge can be life changing. I can think back over my life to several occasions when a key insight about God or myself really hit home. For instance, at one point while I was in seminary, it struck me that all my efforts to manage my sin weren't that impressive to God. Jesus said what matters most is love. The Pharisees were more interested in managing sin than in loving. Jesus was all about awakening people's hearts to love, and within that context sin would be managed. I realized that if I loved God and people, my sin levels would decrease dramatically. That one insight has brought an incredible amount of growth in my life. In the matter of sin management and love, I can say that I "saw the light."

The incarnation story is often misunderstood and is seldom absorbed at any deep personal level. However, it can be like a rich

vein of precious ore. When we mine it and bring it to the surface, it
can be of great value. In fact, the incarnation story contains major
building blocks of the Christian life. Maybe you are a person who
wants to grow as a disciple of Jesus and be transformed. Maybe you
have heard of the incarnation and think it is important but are not
quite sure what to do with it. Maybe you have never felt that you
could grasp why people worship Jesus. Or maybe you are fed up
with being a Christian who lives *for* Jesus and not *with* him. If you
are in one or more of these camps, the incarnation story is for you.
In the hope that you might think more clearly and gain transforming insights about Jesus, this book provides discussion questions for each chapter, gathered at the end of the book. You can
work through these questions on your own or with others.

> *Insights happen as we reflect on God's truth and the Holy Spirit*
> *brings it home to our hearts. Are you hungry for insight about Jesus*
> *and how to live with him? Whether this hunger is strong or faint,*
> *take a few minutes to feel it. Express that feeling to God. Use your*
> *own words or borrow some from Scripture (like Ps 42:1-2, "As the*
> *deer pants for streams of water, so my soul pants for you, my God.*
> *My soul thirsts for God, for the living God"). After you have felt and*
> *expressed your God-hunger for a few minutes, make a vow to allow*
> *your hunger to impel you to pursue God today and in the future.*

Follow the light. If seeing the light is about knowledge, following the light is about action. To follow the light is to act in
such a way that we imitate Jesus. Paul urged the Corinthians,
"Follow my example, as I follow the example of Christ" (1 Cor
11:1). People who shine are active people. Mother Teresa is a great
example. She was known to be a tireless worker, and she expected
a lot from her followers. In the same way, we must put the ways of

Jesus into practice. This is where the rubber meets the road. Day in and day out. Good times or bad times. Busy or taking leisure. Sunday or Monday. Alone or with others. Those who shine most brightly are the ones who practice living with Jesus at this level.

The chapters in this book present core focus areas to practice (for instance, being present with God, humbling ourselves or practicing shalom). Each focus area is rooted in the incarnation story. Within these core focus areas, I have provided a sampling of specific practices to help reinvigorate your life with Jesus. Practices can change, and it is good to be creative. The point is that we maintain a life rich with activities to reinforce and express faith in God and love for the person in front of us. Over time, if we practice living with Jesus habitually, we will be people who shine brightly and consistently.

> *Consider these two groups of people: There are some who say, "Leave us alone! We have no desire to learn your ways" (Job 21:14). And there are others who say, "Show me your ways, LORD. Teach me your paths" (Ps 25:4). If your desire is to be in the latter group, how many of your actions place you there, and how many would place you in the former group? Talk about this with God.*

Imitating Jesus is life-changing. We find ourselves doing things and going places we would never have imagined. We are suddenly making a difference in the world we would have never thought possible. But we don't stop at imitating Jesus. God wants to take us further. He wants Jesus to live through us.

Shine with the light. It is possible to imitate Jesus from a distance, but we can shine with his presence only when he lives in and through us. This is a great mystery. We can explain how to understand Jesus and imitate his deeds. We can exercise a lot of control over those processes. However, living in Jesus' presence is something transcendent that we cannot force or generate. What we can do is put ourselves into the position of allowing God's presence to flow through us. Seeing the light (knowing) and following the light (doing) are building blocks. If we are to shine with the light, we must open ourselves to the presence of the Spirit.

When Jesus shines in us, he does so through the Holy Spirit. Jesus promised that he would not leave us alone but would send the Spirit of God to his disciples, and that the Spirit would teach about and bear witness to Jesus (Jn 15:26). When Jesus appeared to the disciples on Easter, he breathed the Holy Spirit on them (Jn 20:22). It is God's intention to shine through us, and he has provided all the necessary means. Shining is a fresh flow of God's presence, power and peace, and God has made his dwelling within us.

Shining comes not through achievement, production, control and winning but through surrender, prayer and other-centered love. It is a path of giving ourselves more and more deeply to the Spirit's work within us. Often shining is a matter of being ready for the Spirit to move at any point in the day and being open to what the Spirit might want to do. The Spirit might direct us to listen to a person when we don't have time. Or pray for someone instead of enjoying music while we drive. Or rejoice in the midst of suffering. The point is that the Spirit is a living and active presence, and we don't know in advance what he has in mind.

The Holy Spirit is a living and active presence. And the Spirit is with you right now. The Spirit gives you the ability to worship, pray, love, show compassion, forgive, liberate and so on. Take a moment to make yourself ready for the movements of the Spirit in your life today. Open your heart to whatever the Spirit might want to do, even if it is inconvenient, frightening or surprising. Tell God that you want him to do his will through you today.

The indwelling Spirit is the agent of transformation in our lives. God wants to take us from a state of spiritual immaturity, where we sporadically radiate Jesus' presence, to a state of spiritual maturity, where we are ready-made vessels of his grace, love and truth. When we progress along a path of radiating and becoming like Jesus, it is because there is less of us and more of him, so to speak. Progress means that the moments of radiating Christ are sought, recognized, celebrated and multiplied. We can appreciate the moments when we are aware that Jesus is living through us and ask God to multiply them. The good news is that we do not have to have "arrived" at a certain level of Christlikeness to enjoy Jesus' living through us. It can happen now and increase each day.

Prayer Exercise
"Like Stars in the Sky"

At the end of each chapter in this book, I will recommend a prayer exercise to help generate dialogue with God about the ideas in the chapter. Here is an exercise for talking with God about our calling to shine with his presence.

Wait until the sun has gone down and it is fully dark. Go outside, preferably to a place where there is the least amount of light. Stand for a few minutes, pushing all cares to the side and simply being present with the God who is already present with you. When you feel settled, look up into the night sky. See the stars shining against the backdrop of deep darkness. Talk to God about how sin is dark but he is light. Acknowledge to God and yourself that you sometimes participate in the darkness of sin and sometimes participate in his light.

Find a star in the sky that represents the amount of God's brightness your life currently gives off. It might be a star you can barely see, or it might be one that is easily visible. Let that star represent where you currently are in your spiritual life. Now find the brightest star in the sky. Feel your desire to go from being where you are to shining like that brightest star, and talk with God about it. You might close with this prayer: "Jesus, you are the light of the world. Let it be no longer I who live but you who live in me. I want to shine with your light like that brightest star."

PURPOSE

Knowing Why We Are Here

Jesus said, "Peace be with you!
As the Father has sent me, I am sending you."
And with that he breathed on them and
said, "Receive the Holy Spirit."

JOHN 20:21-22

ONE SUMMER AFTERNOON when I was ten years old, my mom interrupted my playtime and called me inside. With a tone of seriousness, she said, "Dave, please walk down to Chet's Market and get us one loaf of bread and one half-gallon of milk. Don't go anywhere else. And please bring me the change." She handed me some cash and sent me on my way.

This was the first time I had ever carried such responsibility. Suddenly I was not just a kid hanging out on a summer day. I was on a mission, sent out to do my mother's will.

Walking to the market on the next block, I noticed new feelings of exhilaration and importance. I was doing this by myself. I was flying solo! I stood a little taller, feeling the responsibility to buy something for the family. This was in a different league from running out to the ice cream truck to get a Fudgsicle.

When I entered the store, my eyes locked onto the Big Hunk bars and then darted to the fresh packs of baseball cards. I remembered my charge and determinedly passed them by. At the end of the aisle, I grabbed a half-gallon milk carton. Then I picked up a loaf of bread. When I returned home, I proudly presented the groceries to my mom and handed her the change. I tried to act like it was no big deal, but I knew I had just done something important. Although I couldn't articulate it at age ten, I felt the sense of meaning that comes with having a purpose that transcends oneself.

Being sent and having a transcendent purpose are the starting points for our journey into a life that shines. We are addressing fundamental human questions: Why am I here? What is the purpose of my life? I couldn't have answered these questions until I devoted myself to Jesus as a young adult. That was when emptiness and searching gave way to focus and meaning. Our lives truly change when we settle the question of why we are here.

COMPETING PURPOSES

Why am I here? There is no more basic human question, and yet most people don't face it head on. They drift, adopting life purposes from experience and culture. "I want to make money and be successful. I want to fall in love with someone special. I also want to make the world a better place. I feel like I should help preserve the environment for future generations. And I want to be comfortable and enjoy myself. To be honest, I'm not sure what is most important. I want it all."

When we are not clear about the purpose of our lives, we absorb a variety of answers from our culture, and because our culture broadcasts so many messages, we can't tell which is more important than the others.

Some people are clear about their purpose, but it is not derived from a commitment to Christ. The drive for money, sex or power commonly consumes people's lives. There are also many more noble purposes in life—political causes, social justice, the environment, fitness and so on. Whether one's purpose is noble or not, people who are highly focused are in the minority.

Finally, there are people whose purpose is following Jesus. Jesus said, "For wide is the gate and broad is the road that leads to destruction, and many enter through it. But small is the gate and narrow the road that leads to life, and only a few find it" (Mt 7:13-14). The road that leads to life is following Jesus. To call Jesus "Lord" (which means "master") is to say, "I am giving up all else to connect with you, learn from you, and obey you." *Following Jesus means allowing him to define our purpose, and that is a fundamental shift—so fundamental that it is referred to as "rebirth" and "conversion."*

Jesus wants our total allegiance. Period. No exceptions. No dilution. To blend other purposes with Jesus is to play a game of double allegiance. In Luke 14, Jesus warned against double allegiance of any kind. Before a large crowd, he said, "If anyone comes to me and does not hate father and mother, wife and children, brothers and sisters—yes, even their own life—such a person cannot be my disciple. And whoever does not carry their cross and follow me cannot be my disciple" (Lk 14:26-27). The word translated "hate" conveys a sense of priorities. To "hate" someone or something in this sense is to prioritize him, her or it at a lower level. Jesus calls us to live with a single purpose, not to add him to the mix of purposes we already have.

Jesus specifically addressed loyalty to family because it was a core value in his culture. Family is a high priority for us as well. Who doesn't want to provide loved ones with an environment of safety and financial opportunity? Indeed, we often expect Jesus to serve those priorities. In Jesus' language, that is to "hate" him and love our families. It is a culturally popular sin. Everything, including our families, our finances and even our own skin, has to be brought under the higher purpose of following Jesus.

When I walked to Chet's, I had one purpose in mind: bring home the milk and bread my mom had sent me to buy. What if I had also wanted to have fun? I would have spent part of the money on what I wanted. I might have bought the milk but chosen a Big Hunk bar and a pack of baseball cards over the bread. I would have failed my mother, disappointed myself and missed the fulfillment of meeting a higher purpose. On a larger scale, that is exactly what Jesus warned us against.

We can picture it another way. Jesus called us to light up the world, but because of sin we operate with a dimmer switch. Mixed allegiances turn down the light. *We are most luminous when we prioritize Jesus first and live single-mindedly.*

Jesus issued an audacious demand, and it might seem unreasonable. But he was not asking people to do anything he was not doing. He was living with one allegiance—to the Father—and one purpose: to do the Father's will. To all of us with double allegiances and mixed purposes, Jesus showed a different way. He *is* a different way.

JESUS MODELED SIMPLICITY AND CLARITY

One of the most important discoveries I have made about Jesus is the clarity he had about his own life. Let's listen in on a conversation from John 3 when Jesus is talking to Nicodemus the Pharisee. Nicodemus had come at night, seeking to understand

Jesus better. In the middle of their conversation, Jesus uttered these famous words: "God so loved the world that he gave his one and only Son, that whoever believes in him shall not perish but have eternal life. For God did not send his Son into the world to condemn the world, but to save the world through him" (Jn 3:16-17). Do you hear Jesus' comments about his purpose? He was well aware that his life was part of an overarching story. Jesus indicated that he was tied to two important reference points: humanity's fall into sin and the Father's sending of his Son to be the Savior.

Jesus viewed being sent on this mission as his defining purpose, and he proclaimed it openly. In John's Gospel, Jesus talks almost incessantly about being sent by the Father, referring to his mission more often than to eternal life.[1] Chapters 3–17 cover the bulk of Jesus' ministry up to his arrest and crucifixion. In those fifteen chapters, Jesus mentions being sent by the Father a striking forty-two times. That's almost three times per chapter! Consider this small sampling of verses:

- Whoever does not honor the Son does not honor the Father, *who sent him*. (Jn 5:23)

- For the works that the Father has given me to finish—the very works that I am doing—testify that *the Father has sent me*. (5:36)

- No one can come to me unless the Father *who sent me* draws them. (6:44)

- I stand with the Father, *who sent me*. (8:16)

- For I did not speak on my own, but the Father *who sent me* commanded me to say all that I have spoken. (12:49)

- Righteous Father, though the world does not know you, I know you, and they know that *you have sent me*. (17:25)

What is John trying to show us in these forty-two quotations? It is surely that Jesus was keenly aware of being sent.

Jesus was clear and settled about his purpose. This is why his opponents found him so difficult. They could not intimidate or manipulate him. Even walking to his death, Jesus remained resolute. This is surely one reason people saw him as a brilliant light. Even in supreme sacrifice, Jesus knew who he was and why he was here. Jesus' example shows that our clarity determines how we face the parts of our faith journey that demand the most sacrifice.

GETTING TO KNOW THE MISSIONARY GOD

Before the church was born, God was on a mission. In his landmark book *The Mission of God*, Old Testament scholar Christopher Wright contends that we should make no mistake—the first missionary was God himself. All our missional activity is merely participation in God's compassionate, outgoing love.

Just a few chapters into the Bible, we see God launching a mission to save the world. God blessed human beings, but when they fell into sin, they doomed themselves to cycles of self-destruction. Moved by compassion, God acted on behalf of all creation. He chose Abraham to be a vessel through whom all nations would be blessed (Gen 12:1-3). The fulfillment and the high point of God's mission was God the Son becoming Jesus the Savior. God wanted to save humanity not by divine fiat but by working within the human race. Wright explains, "And since it was by human hands that sin and evil have invaded life on earth, it would be by human means that God would act to redress it."[2]

God's mission is to save and transform the world. Why "save and transform"? Salvation is often mistakenly portrayed as a removal of guilt and a "ticket to heaven." Being forgiven and being transformed become separated. However, in Scripture salvation is always holistic and transformative. Being "saved" means we are in an active relationship with Jesus, and over years of submitting to him, we are changed down to the core of who we are. This is great news! God forgives *and* transforms us.

Also notice the language of John 3:17—"to save *the world.*" Jesus has nothing less in mind than the salvation of all nations. The divine mission is global in scope. It even extends beyond people to the environment. God rules over all things, and he wants all things to be set right.

Jesus came to save the world from sin and its effects. Sin reaches pervasively into every aspect of our existence, manifesting itself in violent conflict, resentment, abandonment, manipulation, abuse of power and every other malady. Cornelius Plantinga Jr. summarizes sin as any dynamic that disrupts the world from being "the way it ought to be."

So how ought the world be? The biblical vision is shalom. Plantinga describes shalom as: "*universal flourishing, wholeness, and delight*—a rich state of affairs in which natural needs are satisfied and natural gifts fruitfully employed, a state of affairs that inspires joyful wonder as its Creator and Savior opens doors and welcomes the creatures in whom he delights. *Shalom*, in other words, is the way things ought to be."[3] Shalom is a longing at the core of every human heart. It is expressed in every cry to be accepted, loved, forgiven and empowered. It is in every impulse to show compassion and fight for justice.

We can now see more fully why the Son became incarnate: so God could establish shalom throughout the earth. God's mission is to save the world and establish a state of flourishing, wholeness and delight. As the powerful presence of God within humanity, Jesus is our bridge to peace.

GOD'S MISSION GOES VIRAL

When Jesus commissioned his disciples, he released God's saving and transforming love to spread throughout the world. Let's return to the incarnation narrative for another key vignette. John 20 tells us that following Jesus' death, the disciples shut themselves in a room, locking the door for fear that the Jewish authorities would burst in to arrest them. However, the one who suddenly appeared in the room was not a Jewish officer but Jesus himself. The disciples were understandably shocked. Jesus said, "Peace be with you!" and showed them his wounds. However, he was there for a greater purpose than restoring contact with his disciples. Jesus had come to inaugurate a new era in the divine mission, essentially kicking it into a higher gear. Repeating his blessing, he said, "Peace be with you! As the Father has sent me, so I am sending you." Then he breathed on them and said, "Receive the Holy Spirit" (Jn 20:21-22).

In this one crucial scene, Jesus performed two interrelated acts of sending. Jesus sent the Holy Spirit to the disciples, and he sent the disciples into the world. All the disciples' preparation had led to this climactic point. They were now carriers of the divine presence, participating in the divine mission. When they received the Spirit, they became like torches, spreading light everywhere there was darkness.

This episode in the upper room becomes a decisive turning point in the story of God's mission. Jesus is sent to live, die and rise again as a human being. When Jesus departs from this world to take his place at the right hand of the Father, the mission continues, now with the potential to spread around the world. It is like a video that gets posted on the Internet and goes viral by passing from person to person. When Jesus sent the Spirit upon the disciples and sent the disciples into the world, the divine mission was released to go viral. Indeed, going viral is exactly what the kingdom is supposed to do.

THE ASTOUNDING TRUTH ABOUT OUR LIVES

There is no greater cause than giving ourselves so other broken people might flourish as they find life in God. But Christians can lose sight of the greatness of this calling. The truth is, we don't *have* to do this; we *get* to do this. Grasping the far-reaching greatness of God's mission can fill us with a meaningful sense of direction. Jesus said, "I have come that they may have life, and have it to the full" (Jn 10:10). Being given a life purpose that shines brilliantly with meaning is part of the abundant life—that is, life that is invigorating and has an impact.

Yet we can be our own worst enemies. "Human beings are escape artists," observes pastor Danielle Shroyer. We feel vulnerable and fragile, and we grasp at ways of empowering and protecting ourselves. We can even spin the biblical story to be a tale of escape *from* the world instead of engagement *with* it.

Sometimes I wonder why God chose to involve us in his mission. "Really? You want to use us to accomplish your purposes? Do you know what we're like?" Of course he does. Despite our weaknesses—indeed, in the midst of our weaknesses—God gives us the privilege of working toward the salvation of the world. We simultaneously work out our own salvation (Phil 2:12) and participate in the world's salvation. This act of empowerment is one of the most astounding truths of the Bible. I have seen my life and the lives of many others change when we recognize God's mission as the greatest cause on earth.

God's will for our lives is laced with mystery. Yet exchanging our small ideas for God's transcendent ideas is well worth it. I once saw a bookmark advertising a book with the slogan "This marks the end of your perfect little world." Exactly! The world I construct on my own will be manageable and small-minded. It *needs* to come to an end. To be sent is to give up my "perfect little world" and follow Jesus into the "great unknown." The great unknown is a path only God knows, leading to a future that unleashes greatness that only God can imagine. Our world is desperate for people who can lead others into this great unknown—people who have grown from "only the strongest survive" into "only the strongest give life to others."

People who are surrendering to God show us that it's possible. Through reading, connect with one or two people who are inspiring examples. If you aren't sure whom to read about, I suggest starting with Jesus, especially as he is presented in the Gospel of John. The apostle Paul was also keenly aware of being sent, and we can read about it in Acts 9, Acts 13 and following, and his short letter to the Galatians. A more contemporary example is Mother Teresa. She describes her sense of mission well in Mother Teresa: Come Be My Light, *edited by Brian Kolodiejchuk.*

FIVE WAYS TO BECOME PEOPLE OF PURPOSE

Becoming a person of purpose means making a core commitment, which then gives birth to countless choices ranging from minute to life-altering. The depth of our commitment to Jesus is always on display. The truth is told through our actions. A weak commitment leads to choices that blend in with our culture, whereas a strong commitment turns up the light of Jesus' presence.

Zacchaeus is a biblical example. Luke tells us that Zacchaeus was a chief tax collector, which means he collected commissions from the tax collectors who worked under him (Lk 19). He was one of the wealthiest citizens of Jericho, but he was disdained as a Roman collaborator and swindler. One day Jesus passed through Jericho, and he noticed Zacchaeus. Crossing social boundaries, Jesus visited Zacchaeus for dinner. The tax collector responded powerfully to Jesus' gesture of grace. He immediately gave half of his estate to the poor. Out of the remaining half, he vowed that, if he had cheated anyone, he would pay back four times the amount. Seeing the change in Zacchaeus's heart, Jesus exclaimed, "Today salvation has come to this house" (Lk 19:9).

Giving half of his estate to the poor and making such generous restitution would surely have made Zacchaeus unique among chief tax collectors. These were the radical actions of one who felt the undeserved shock of grace and responded by devoting everything to God.

> *If you have never done it before, or even if you have, turn control of your life over to God. He has much better ideas than you do. Surrender yourself to his purposes. You can start by praying Hebrews 10:7. In this verse, the writer of Hebrews quotes Psalm 40 in reference to Jesus' surrender: "Then I said, 'Here I am—it is written about me in the scroll—I have come to do your will, my God.'" Pray these words along with Jesus and surrender to God's will.*

Living our core commitment to Jesus is a daily walk. Following are five ways we can deepen our commitment to Jesus and shine in the small choices of daily life.

Surrender—and keep surrendering. Jesus often reminded his hearers that he wasn't operating by his own will but by the will of the One who sent him (Jn 5:30). Surrendering to God is at the core of biblical spirituality. And trust me, sooner or later God will test you to see whether you will surrender a whole range of things you might care about—making money, falling in love, having a family, living in the right house, being safe and so on.

A core commitment to Jesus shows up in every part of life. On the morning I write this, I am experiencing some minor friction with a friend. I can react out of frustration or trust Jesus to breathe his grace into the situation. Living our core commitment to Jesus is made of moments like this.

Embed yourself in a like-minded community. We're apt to become like those we're around. If you spend lots of time with self-determined people, it'll be harder for you to transition from self-determined to sent. Conversely, as you embed yourself in a community of people who are aware of being sent, you'll find yourself encouraged by, and actively encouraging, those people. You will meet people who can be examples to follow. Being around such people helps us visualize ourselves doing something similar and helps keep us going.

> You can also connect with a person in your community who's focused on God's mission. Ask him or her to describe the sense of mission and times of struggles. Ask for advice on how you can focus more on God's mission.
>
> Write down your thoughts. Share them with an individual or small group. Talk together about God's mission, the simplicity of knowing why we are here and what choices you might want to make. Commit to action in one another's presence.

Change your vocabulary. How we go from accepting our culture's priorities to committing ourselves to God's mission relates significantly to how we talk. Frankly, many of us need to change our vocabulary. If we believe we're sent, we need to talk like it. Here's one example of a change we can make. Jesus frequently referred to God as "the one who sent me." Try referring to Jesus as "the one who sent us." See how it opens up new conversations with people and how it creates a shift in how you think of God and yourself.

> Review the verses noted in this chapter where Jesus mentions being sent by the Father.[4] Try referring to Jesus as "the one who sent us" and yourself as "a shalom-seeker." What happens as you practice this new vocabulary? Talk to God about being sent. Memorize John 20:21-22 and make it a daily interaction with God to put yourself in the disciples' place, being sent by Jesus and receiving the Holy Spirit from him.

Stretch yourself. This is common sense, but it is also established practice in psychological therapy: if you want to live differently, put yourself in situations where you have to act differently. Psychotherapists often help a client replace his or her destructive self-identity with a healthier one. Many encourage these clients to enter social situations that are incompatible with their old self-identity. For instance, let's say Steven struggles with a self-perception that he's irresponsible and worthless. His therapist would likely coach him to enter situations where he must show some responsibility.

Similarly, if we want to see ourselves as sent, we should put ourselves in situations that demand we act accordingly. When we practice being sent, the Holy Spirit permeates our hearts with truth as if he were kneading dough. The Spirit presses, folds and works the truth within us. Feeding the homeless and going on a mission trip are good examples of putting ourselves in stretching situations that can stimulate thinking of ourselves in a new light. In the everyday world, we can perform simple acts of love. The more we find ourselves doing so, the more we adopt a new identity as people on a mission.

> *Do three deeds today, small or large, for no other reason than that this is your purpose. To go deeper, make "three deeds" a daily assignment for the next month.*

Stay close to God. You may be able to get through your day reasonably well without talking to God much. It depends what your goals are. If your top priorities are things like making money, being successful, finding love, passing your classes, being involved in worthy social causes and so on, then you can get by without depending on God at any deep level. But if you want to live out God's mission, you *need* God all day every day.

For Jesus to really live out his mission, he had to stay closely connected to his Father, who had sent him. He wanted his disciples to live the same way. In John 15:1-8, Jesus indicates that we are to "remain" in him because, he says, "apart from me you can do nothing." When it comes to bearing fruit—experiencing God's saving love flowing through us—we must remain in communion with God.

It's pretty simple. *Jesus is the light. You are not. If you want to shine, Jesus must shine through you.* Making yourself a better vessel for God's light means depending on Jesus.

WHAT IF

Who are we as Christians? If we were to ask that question in Christian circles, we might hear answers like "We are sinners who are saved by grace" or "We are God's adopted children" or maybe "We are God's beloved." What we wouldn't commonly hear is "We are people sent on God's mission." The idea that we are sent might register in our heads, but it hasn't soaked into our bones. What if it did? What if being sent came to register so deeply that it became part of our identity? There are men and women among us who've come to this point. They're people of clarity who make uncommon choices and inspire those around them. You may know one of these people. You are called to *be* one of these people.

The rest of this book builds on a fundamental choice: setting God's mission as the highest purpose in our lives and acting accordingly. When we set our wills to be people of purpose, our hearts are better prepared for God to shine through us.

Prayer Exercise
"So I Am Sending You"

John 20 paints a vivid picture. Read it all the way through. Then quiet yourself in prayer as you prepare to focus on John 20:19-20. Read these two verses slowly, pausing over every image and every element of the encounter that unfolds. Place yourself in the story as one of the disciples. What does the room look like? Who is there? What do you feel before Jesus is present? When Jesus enters the room, what is it like? What do you feel as he greets you, shows you his wounds and stands among his friends? As you absorb the elements of this story, open your heart to the presence of Jesus right here, right now.

Now slowly read verse 21. How do you feel being commissioned by Jesus? Be specific. What about this inspires you? What causes you to want to hold back?

Move to verse 22. What do you envision happening when the disciples received the Holy Spirit? Invite Jesus to breathe his Spirit on you in this present moment.

Finally, read verse 23. What kind of responsibility is Jesus giving the disciples? How does it make you feel to know that we have that level of responsibility? Talk to God about how it makes you feel to participate in God's grace and forgiveness.

In closing this prayer time, ask God to clarify his mission in your life. Wait on him to show you some specific things you can do to bring his saving and transforming love to the world.

BEING PRESENT WITH GOD

*All this took place to fulfill what the Lord had said through
the prophet: "The virgin will conceive and give birth
to a son, and they will call him Immanuel"
(which means "God with us").*

MATTHEW 1:22-23

N THE MIDST OF A SPIRITED DISCUSSION, my wife and I agreed we needed to reinvigorate our relationship. We had been married for more than twenty years, and we had poured a great deal of effort into navigating our work lives and parenting children. Over time we had slipped into a pattern of being comanagers of our household. Most of our discussions revolved around not what was happening in our hearts but the commitments on this week's calendar and who was going to do what. We agreed we needed to become friends again. Making that decision and following through on it has breathed life into our marriage.

Something similar has to happen in our relationship with God. Rather than treating him like a comanager of our lives (which is wrong on more than one level), we need to give our hearts to him and become friends with him. We need to walk in the footsteps of Brother Lawrence.

Brother Lawrence came from the lower class of seventeenth-century France, but he became influential for one reason: he learned how to commune with God all through the day. This simple practice affected him so profoundly that he saw it as the key that unlocks the whole spiritual life. Through it he experienced a steady stream of delights, some of which were so intense that he had to find ways to suppress his reactions.

He described himself as "a great awkward fellow who broke everything."[1] He was not educated, so when he joined a monastery in Paris, he was destined for a menial position. For many years he served in the kitchen. With its clatter and bustle, it seemed an odd training ground for prayer. Yet he learned to enjoy God's presence there as much as when he was chanting a psalm with his brothers in chapel. He had found the sweetness of ongoing communion with God, which is at the heart of shining with Jesus' presence.

The power of Brother Lawrence's approach was its humility and simplicity. He believed we are not worthy of God's attention, but God is always with us nonetheless. Over years of practice, Brother Lawrence developed a habit of doing all things to please God. Even a small action like picking up a piece of straw could be an offering of love.

Despite his low position, he became a person others sought out for spiritual counsel. "Wherever he was, the Light was there. . . . He showed us how, at any given moment and in any given circumstance, the soul that seeks God may find him, and practice the presence of God."[2] He died at age eighty, "full of love and honored by all who knew him, leaving behind a name which has been 'as precious as ointment poured forth.'"[3]

Bringing light to the world and living in continual communion with God is not just for legendary Christians. It is the normal calling for all of us. However, we get caught in an inner tug-of-war. On one side, we believe God is present and active, always and everywhere. On the other side, we get caught up in a fast-paced and demanding life, and we don't remember to involve God. Live *with* Jesus; live *for* Jesus—this tug-of-war goes on constantly. We must live *with* him if we want to go from glowing dimly to shining brightly.

GOD WITH US

One of the most important themes in the Bible is Immanuel— "God with us." From cover to cover, God assures people he is here, yet they struggle with faith. Sometimes he makes his presence well known, but other times he seems absent. God is patient, because he knows that living by faith in a God we can't see, in the midst of a world that presents so many challenges, is tough to do.

In the creation story, God was with Adam and Eve. Even after they had fallen into sin, God came looking for them in the garden. Outside the garden, as human civilization began, God pursued the first people. God pursued Noah. God pursued Abraham, Isaac and Jacob. God pursued the people of Israel through Moses. Notably, on Mount Sinai, God did not say to Moses, "Stay here with me on this mountain." Rather, he said, "I will be with you." God continued to pursue the people of Israel through Joshua, Samuel, David and the prophets. When Jesus was born, it was the quintessential expression of God going out to humanity. He had now pursued us even to the point of becoming one of us.

Although the idea that God is with us is a key biblical theme, the name Immanuel appears rarely in Scripture—in Isaiah 7:14 and 8:8, and Matthew 1:23 (quoting Isaiah). The presence of God that is communicated in the name Immanuel is a central element in the incarnation story.

Isaiah 7:14 is often quoted around Christmastime: "The virgin will conceive and give birth to a son, and will call him Immanuel." The verse is warm with hope, but the original story is tragic. It was the eighth century before Christ, and Ahaz ruled Judah, the southern kingdom. There was grave concern. The northern kingdom of Israel and the nearby kingdom of Aram had formed an alliance against Judah, and they were planning to attack Jerusalem. Ahaz was entering into a classic test of faith.

Ahaz didn't like the option of fighting on his own. Israel and Aram were too strong. There was another political option. Beyond Aram to the northeast loomed the superpower Assyria. Ahaz could reach out to Assyria for help.

Enter the prophet Isaiah bringing a third, unexpected option. God wanted Ahaz to rely only on him. Knowing Ahaz was not strong in faith, God offered a miraculous sign: "The virgin will conceive and give birth to a son, and will call him Immanuel" (Is 7:14). The name of the baby means "God is with us."

Ahaz was not swayed. He appealed to Assyria, making Judah Assyria's vassal and sending treasures from God's temple as a gift. He "acted as though God is not and Assyria is"—a tragic and foolish choice.[4] The notorious superpower rolled over first Aram and then Israel. Unfortunately Assyria would cause the eventual undoing of Judah. Ahaz serves as an example of the consequences of acting as if God is absent.

Let's fast-forward through the Scriptures to Matthew. In telling the story of Jesus' birth, Matthew carefully highlights two names. Both communicate important truths. First, an angel directed Joseph to give the baby the name Jesus, which means "savior." The angel explained, "He will save his people from their sins" (Mt 1:21).

Second, Matthew adds another name for Jesus: "All this took place to fulfill what the Lord had said through the prophet: 'The virgin will conceive and give birth to a son, and they will call him Immanuel' (which means 'God with us')" (Mt 1:22-23). As far we know, no one ever directly called Jesus by the name Immanuel. Matthew is teaching that Jesus was the fulfillment of Isaiah's prophecy and that "in Jesus none less than God came right where we are." Furthermore, "at the end of this Gospel there is the promise that Jesus will be with his people to the end of the age (28:20)—God is with us indeed."[5]

Matthew is the only New Testament writer to connect Isaiah 7:14 to Jesus. However, he makes a point that resonates throughout the entire New Testament. Jesus was not just a man. He was the very presence of God, walking and talking among us, saving us, showing us how to live and uniting us with God. Matthew pauses over this point, wanting his readers to understand one of the most essential aspects of the Jesus story—that *in the person of Jesus, God became present in our world in an unprecedented way, and he was here to save us.*

The story of God's presence with humanity did not stop with Jesus. When the church was born, Jesus sent the Holy Spirit to his followers. Through the church, God is reaching out to the ends of the earth. All of God's reaching out attains its fulfillment in the age to come. Revelation 21–22 paints a picture of the New Jerusalem, the jewel of the new heavens and the new earth. As the city descends from heaven, a voice from the throne proclaims, "Look! God's dwelling place is now among the people, and he will dwell with them. They will be his people, and God himself will be with them and be their God" (Rev 21:3). God does not pull us up to heaven. He makes his home here. In the meantime, while we wait for those events to happen, the final words of the Bible are "The grace of the Lord Jesus be *with God's people.* Amen" (Rev 22:21).

Although God is with us, human beings have a hard time responding. There are two fundamentally different theologies— "God is absent" and "God is present." In the former, God is far off and not substantially involved in our lives. He may exist, but he doesn't do much. He leaves us on our own to negotiate life the best we can. In the latter—the story of Immanuel—God pursues us in order to dwell with us.

The theology we adopt shapes how we relate to God, make decisions, raise our children, manage our money, pursue our career, approach romantic relationships and everything else in life. These two ways of life are as different as darkness is from light. I will call one *practicing God's absence* and the other *practicing God's presence.*

PRACTICING GOD'S ABSENCE

In a nutshell, practicing God's absence is about living as if God were uninvolved and irrelevant to everyday life. It means operating with little or no conscious, receptive, trusting connection to God. Author Parker Palmer coined the term "functional atheism" to describe someone who believes in God but lives as if he didn't exist. The functional atheist talks a good game about God but inwardly believes that if anything good is going to happen, we must make it happen.[6]

In the Western world, self-reliance is woven into our cultural heritage and instilled in us from an early age. Our scientific worldview removes God from the natural world, and we are taught to rely on human resources. For me, practicing God's absence is almost effortless. Even when I am deliberately trying to pay attention to God, I can easily go through large portions of the day with little or no intentional connection with him. It seems almost natural to compartmentalize life into prayerful and nonprayerful zones. Prayerful zones include my morning devotions and gatherings in which I am praying with other Christians. Nonprayerful zones include everything else—working, playing, being entertained, paying the bills, driving, answering emails, shuttling my kids and so on. I am so prone to be independent from God that as a pastor, I can practice God's absence even while preparing sermons, leading meetings and giving spiritual counsel.

In his book *The Christian Atheist*, pastor Craig Groeschel speaks candidly about his own history of practicing God's absence. Groeschel characterizes it as an addiction from which he is recovering. He points out that Christian Atheists are everywhere. "They attend Catholic churches, Baptist churches, Pentecostal churches, nondenominational churches, and even churches where the pastor says, 'GAW-duh!' when he's preaching. They attend big seminaries, Big Ten universities, and every college in between. They are every age and race and occupation—and some even read their Bibles every day."[7] Practicing God's absence is a serious problem, even among Christians.

Practicing God's absence is connected with humanity's fall into sin. The account of the fall in Genesis 3 is a story of spiritual separation. Adam and Eve decide to assert their independence from God. Eating the fruit was a monumental event that was both self-exalting and self-defeating. *Whenever we find ourselves forgetting God and living independently from him, the story of the fall is being replayed in our lives.*

Practicing God's absence doesn't just separate us from God's blessings. It also gives rise to all manner of misbehavior and incurs God's discipline. When someone has wronged us, we stew over it and plot ways to get even. When money is tight, we fret and lose sleep. When lust comes calling, we rationalize why giving in this time is okay. When practicing God's absence becomes our life-style, we sow our own destruction.

Practicing God's absence takes different forms in different cultures. In the Western world, the growing norm is to fill up every available minute with some kind of activity. Multitasking is a necessity. We work, text, email, check social media and eat—all at the same time. We have become chronic overschedulers and technology addicts who are uneasy without a steady stream of stimulation. *This overcharged pace of life numbs us to God's presence and leads us to practice God's absence.*

Recently during morning devotions I was fessing up to some failures in my life, one of which was a sense of apathy about God and what he was doing within me. I was reading in Psalm 145 that God is gracious and compassionate, slow to anger and rich in love. How could I be apathetic about *that?* In the context of praying over these things, I noticed that my drift into spiritual numbness had corresponded with a period of hurry. Hurry had exacerbated my preexisting tendency to practice God's absence, and practicing God's absence had numbed my spirit.

Closely akin to overactivity is information overload. The volume of information available to us is exponentially greater than in any previous period of human history. Correspondingly, the amount of information we consume has skyrocketed. Information overload takes its toll on us. "What information consumes is rather obvious: it consumes the attention of its recipients," says economist Herbert Simon. "Hence, a wealth of information creates a poverty of attention."[8] We think of ourselves as consumers, but in the age of information overload, we have become the consumed.

Yet experts argue that we can't simply blame our problems on overabundance of information.[9] The onus is on us to control our intake of information. There are two sins that are alarmingly pervasive in contemporary Christian culture. First is Infogluttony—gorging oneself on information the way a gluttonous eater gobbles food. The symptom of Infogluttony is devoting more energy to consuming information *about* God (blogs, social media, online sermons, books, magazines, videos, etc.) than communing *with* God. *The fact is, the amount of Christian information we take in may be harming our relationship with God.*

Second is the rise of the Attention-Deficit Christian—someone who loves and trusts God, but whose attention is consumed by information so that he or she is less capable of paying full attention to people or God. The Attention-Deficit Christian unwittingly practices God's absence by failing to govern the craving for stimulation in the swirling cloud of teachings, opinions and comments. We should not think God will overlook our disconnection from him and others because we were filling ourselves with information about him.

Take ten minutes to assess honestly and prayerfully your attachment to information and use of electronic devices. Are you Infogluttonous? Do you tend to be an Attention-Deficit Christian? Let God speak to you about those issues. What action might he want you to take? Consider going on an information fast where you unplug for a day or longer and spend that time connecting with God.

Our fallenness, our pace of life and information overload—these are all factors that lead us to live as if either God didn't exist or he were not a meaningful factor in the everyday world. Practicing

God's absence is the dominant lifestyle in the Western world. It sucks light out of us, creating dark hollows within our souls.

PRACTICING GOD'S PRESENCE

Practicing God's absence can feel natural, but beneath our tendency to drift into self-reliance is a deep longing for communion with God. The longing comes from both us and God. We are created to connect with God, and God pulls us toward himself. Richard Foster writes, "Today the heart of God is an open wound of love. . . . He longs for our presence."[10]

God is already present with us. The question is whether we will be present with him. I have been helped by frequent meditation on the story of the incarnation, a powerful statement of God's presence. If our desire to walk with God fills a thimble, his desire to walk with us fills an ocean. Through Jesus walking among us and then giving us the Holy Spirit, the story loudly proclaims "Immanuel—God is with us!" Practicing God's presence is simply cooperating with the God who is already here, welcoming us with open arms. It is holding God in an ongoing conversation at all times, even during temptation and suffering.

Whereas practicing God's absence requires no effort, practicing God's presence is a learned way of life. Brother Lawrence described it as "the schooling of the soul to find its joy in His Divine Companionship." In school we learn to do things we didn't previously know how to do. No one shows up to the school of prayer as a graduate. Nor is there any "testing out" so we can skip grade levels. We grow in prayer by learning, practicing and persevering through our failures.

Oswald Chambers said that just as our bodies are nourished by food, God's life within us is nourished by prayer. We can feed this new life or we can starve it. Likewise missionary Frank Laubach held that practicing God's presence is a central element of Christian discipleship, not an accessory. If Jesus carried an on-going conversation with his Father, then so should his followers. Alas, if this is essential to being a Christian, then Laubach feared there are few good Christians.[11] It isn't that practicing God's presence is impossible. It's that few Christians try it, and fewer stick with it until it becomes part of who they are. Few shine this brightly. I am absolutely dead set on being among those few. I am "all in" for knowing God as few know him and living with God as few live with him. How about you?

> Especially after she became famous, Mother Teresa had one of the most demanding schedules on earth. Yet she had ways of remaining in God's presence whether she was praying at the Eucharist, tending to a dying man, or conducting an interview. One tool she used was this: Stop for a moment before you begin your next activity and devote yourself and the activity to God. Try it now. Before you read the next paragraph, devote yourself to God in love. Do this as many times as you can throughout the day.

Practicing God's presence is challenging, but it comes with a huge payoff. We become close companions of God. No matter what is going on around us, we trust God, overflow with his love, hope in him and participate with him so he may be glorified. We begin to recognize his presence everywhere. Learning this way of life can be summed up in two stages, which I call "training" and "treasuring."

Training. Brother Lawrence said it took him ten years of persistent practice before he experienced a breakthrough, after which his communion with God was consistently rich. It's good to know up front that this is a lifetime practice for us, and there is no substitute for sheer persistence. In this "schooling of the soul," we are not overcoming God's reluctance to abide with us. Quite the opposite. We are overcoming our ingrained sinful patterns of depending on ourselves and remaining distant from God. Training is about rewiring the way we do life.

Brother Lawrence recommended that people begin with a formal commitment. It might sound like this: "Holy God, you are more loving to me than I could ever deserve. I am responding by making it my only business in this life to please you. From now on, I am determined always to be with you, to love you and to honor you. I am going to do this all through each day. When I stumble and fall, please pick me up. I will not be able to do any of this without your help. Here I am, Father. Let's begin."

Next we start building a habit of continually directing ourselves to God. What does that look like in practice? It is *an ongoing conversation with God and an immediate responsiveness to his will.* This practice doesn't rely on methods or techniques. It's not about making big speeches to God. It is profoundly simple. Worship him with a word. Ask for his grace. Devote yourself to him with an uncomplicated prayer like "Here I am, Lord. I want to do your will." Trying to be fancy will only distract you from God.

Laubach committed himself in all his waking moments to listen to the inner voice of God and ask, "Father, what would you like to say or do in this moment?" I often simply say, "Yes, Lord," meaning that I acknowledge his presence, submit to him as Lord and say yes to whatever he wants to do. Want to get simpler still? Don't use words. Silently direct your desire to God. We can pray like this in a moment, even while we're busy doing something that requires our attention.

If we are to follow God's leading throughout the day, we must be familiar with what he is likely to do. What is God like? What does he care about? What does he often do? What does he *not* do? The more I know about God, the easier it is to discern what he might like to say or do in any given moment. Reading and reflecting on Scripture is key to practicing God's presence.

This practice doesn't put demands on our schedules. It goes on constantly and underlies everything we do. Once a friend was lamenting that her schedule is packed and she has almost no time for prayer. I understood all too well what she was struggling with, but I saw another side of the issue. I thought, *Yes, you do! You have every waking moment to pray. Praying doesn't take any time at all.* Sitting down to have focused prayer sessions is part of our prayer life, but so is praying all day long while we do other things.

Communing with God becomes easier with prayer cues. Identify an object you use every day—for example, your toothbrush. Wrap a rubber band around its handle as a reminder to commune with God every time you brush your teeth. If you brush your teeth in the morning and evening, talk to him about the day just beginning or coming to an end. You can love him as your Creator and treat each brushstroke as a thank offering for your physical body. Start with brushing your teeth prayerfully and build from there to other daily activities. Tell someone how it is affecting you.

Over time we grow accustomed to practicing God's presence and loving him for his sake. Progress is by small degrees, and setbacks are common. Especially in the beginning, we often forget to practice God's presence. When this happens, we confess our weakness to God and admit we can't do this without him. We move on in peace. We allow ourselves to fail over and over, and we allow God to be gracious toward us. We don't give up. Like Laubach, we resolve and then re-resolve to live closely with God.

One popular tool is the use of short prayers throughout the day. They can be repetitive or not. It doesn't matter. Choose a word or phrase that recenters you on God. Just breathing the name "Jesus" can shift your attitude in the blink of an eye. Or "beloved." Or "Lord." Or the classic "Lord Jesus, have mercy on me, a sinner." These prayers are designed to refocus our hearts on God's presence instantaneously. Experiment with breath prayers this week to help you practice God's presence.

Some days are easy, and some are difficult. Yesterday I was attentive to God for much of the day, and I experienced his grace. As I listened to him, I felt I needed to cancel an appointment. An hour later, out of the blue my teenage son asked if we could spend some time together. I rejoiced that God had dropped this priceless gift into my day. Yet today is another story. I woke up tired, and I am struggling to maintain contact with God. I am offering him what I can give today as well as praying he gives me strength to offer more. I want to beat myself up for failing, but I know that doesn't help. And quitting isn't an option. So I keep returning to him in a disjointed pattern of remembering-forgetting-remembering-forgetting-remembering. On days like this, I am supremely grateful for God's grace. I also believe God especially appreciates our meager offerings on the tough days.

Brother Lawrence was emphatic about motives. Especially in the beginning, we want to please God, but we are also in it for ourselves, hoping to experience God's benefits. Lawrence exhorts us to put to death any self-orientation. We must train ourselves to *love God for his sake alone.* Failing to make the transition from self-centeredness to God-centeredness is what holds many Christians back from spiritual maturity.

Treasuring. As we develop the holy habit of practicing God's presence, his love shines in our hearts in a new way. He becomes our deepest treasure, and we cannot help but commune with him. *Treasuring is the reward for those who persist through training.*

To be more specific, Richard Foster says that through training, we notice three types of change within us. First, prayer sinks into our unconscious mind. We pray without really being fully focused on it. "Breathed longings of wonder and adoration seem always underneath and in the background of everything—a little like a tune that we suddenly realize we have been humming all day long."[12] Second, prayer moves into the heart. "Our prayer becomes more and more tender, more and more loving, more and more spontaneous. It feels less like work and more like delight."[13] We are more tender toward other people and their needs. Finally, prayer permeates one's whole personality. It was said of Francis of Assisi that he "seemed not so much a man praying as prayer itself made man."[14] One of my deepest prayers is that someday I will reach this final stage. I catch glimpses of it that keep me moving forward.

Practicing God's presence has a radical effect on our hearts. We notice God giving us gifts all day long. A meal. An unexpected smile. A feeling of joy. There are few better ways to overcome sin in our lives than to devote ourselves to God all through the day. For example, I am prone to worry about things—my job, marriage, kids, finances, you name it. However, I have found it impossible to worry when I am practicing God's presence. In place of worry there is peaceful trust. The same can be said for other temptations like taking revenge, lusting or blowing up in anger. They aren't compatible with a loving, trusting, hoping communion with God.

> One of my friends has found giving thanks to be the greatest difference maker in his prayer life. He has long wanted to live more consistently in God's presence, but it wasn't until he made a habit of giving thanks that he experienced breakthroughs. Start with giving thanks while showering or driving to work. Do this every day for two weeks, and talk with someone about the results.

As we advance, we notice that prayer is not something we "make happen." It takes on a passive dimension. An older friend who is advanced in prayer told me that at this stage of his life, prayer is less about what he says to God and more about what he receives from God. He experiences prayer as an active, loving awareness. Brother Lawrence said the external activities he was involved in made no difference in his connection with God. Washing dishes or having devotions—he communed with God equally at all times.

Practicing God's presence follows a general spiritual principle: *God gives us what we really want.* Too often we content ourselves with the goods of this world. If we really want God, he will give himself to us in ways that are tailored just for us. However, we have to leave behind lesser attachments and seek God. "You will seek me and find me when you seek me with all your heart" (Jer 29:13).

Prayer Exercise
Start a 90-Day Experiment with God

Missionary Frank Laubach conducted an experiment: what would happen if he tried to commune with God all the time?

The practice changed his life. In Laubach's spirit of experimentation, try this over the next ninety days. For the first thirty days, return to God at least every hour. You might want to set reminders for yourself using a cell phone, a computer or other cues. For the second thirty days, every fifteen minutes. For the final thirty days, try every five minutes.

Success isn't being perfect. Success is loving God with a little more of your heart, soul, mind and strength than you did yesterday. It is overcoming your tendency to practice God's absence and instead settling into a lifelong habit of practicing God's presence. Try it and talk with others about your journey.

BEING PRESENT IN OUR BODIES

The Word became flesh and

made his dwelling among us.

JOHN 1:14

'M A PRETTY PHYSICAL PERSON. I need to be active. When I don't exercise for a couple of days, I get cranky. I can't sleep. I get hot flashes. I don't want to be around people. On the other hand, when I do exercise, I feel great. There's the endorphin rush right after the workout, and then for hours after that there is the satisfying feeling of muscles recovering from strenuous activity. That is a rewarding sensation. It is also rewarding to enjoy the good night's sleep that comes after a hard workout.

I like to be outside. At one church where I worked, I was known as "the walking pastor," because I liked to walk and talk. Hey, our church offices were two blocks from the beach in Southern California. Why talk inside when you can soak in the beauty of the beach, smell the salty air and hear the breaking waves? I love being out in the fresh air. I live in Sacramento now, and one of the things I appreciate about local culture is that everyone seems to want to be outside walking, running, riding bikes, rafting on the river, going to the park, getting out to the nearby mountains and so on.

Whether you would consider yourself active or not, you are also a physical person. We are continually aware of how we feel, what we look like, how our clothes fit, what foods sound good, and what we are able to do and not do. In Western culture, we are trained to pay a lot of attention to our bodies. We make decisions about what to eat and what not to eat. We talk about the importance of physical exercise. In fact, we can't watch television without seeing a host of ads for exercise programs and weight-loss schemes.

Beyond our own bodies, people's bodies in general are a continual subject of conversation. Starting in middle school, boys and girls talk in all sorts of appropriate and inappropriate ways about bodies—their own, each other's and everyone else's. As adults, we are fascinated with the bodies of celebrities. You can't stand in line to pay for your groceries without seeing at least half a dozen photos of celebrities splashed on the covers of tabloid magazines. This actress shows off her perfect body at a Jamaican beach. That actress suddenly looks twenty pounds overweight. This actor has been lifting weights. That one looks as if he hasn't slept in days. Our bodies and everyone else's bodies are a preoccupation in our culture.

And I haven't even mentioned sexuality. Talk about a cultural obsession.

If our bodies are such an important part of human life and an ongoing preoccupation of our culture, then the church is leading the way in clarifying the role of our bodies in the spiritual life, right? Not exactly. Recently I asked a friend what the church usually teaches about the role of the physical body in the Christian life.

She asked, "Oh, you mean the body of Christ?"

I replied, "No, I mean our physical bodies."

She paused and looked away, searching for a connection. Then she offered, "Umm, you mean like how we are the hands and feet of Christ?"

"Well, kind of." I pinched the skin on my forearm. "I mean our flesh and bones. What have you heard the church teach about the role of our bodies in living out our faith?"

She shook her head. "I don't think I have ever heard the church talk about that."

I was struck by her answer, but it wasn't a complete surprise. The general tone in the church has been either disdain for the body or a general avoidance of the subject. No wonder Christians don't know exactly what to think about the body!

The disconnect between the church's teaching and our physical bodies is ironic, given that our faith emphasizes God's intentional physicality: "the Word became *flesh* and made his dwelling among us" (Jn 1:14). God became flesh—human flesh. Stop and think about that for a minute. It is incredible that the Creator of all worlds would clothe himself in our flesh and invest himself in this insignificant planet. God in human skin. Human skin on God. I don't believe we really grapple with the idea often enough. But if God's love for us is so great that he did even this, then it ought to affect the way we approach living in our own skin.

As I thought about my friend's answer, I reflected on questions that go unaddressed when we don't talk about our bodies. Is my body a detriment to my relationship with God? Does it matter what I do with my body? What are the connections between my body and my spirituality?

I replied to my friend, "There is a lot to learn about how being a Christian is a physical way of life."

She raised her eyebrows. "I would like to hear more about that."

MIXED MESSAGES

If we listen to what the church says about the body, we are likely to hear one of three messages: "escape the body," "ignore the body" or "flourish in the body." The first two separate the body from the soul. The third searches for a holistic approach to the human person.

Escape the body. A long time ago I was in a prayer group strictly for the spiritually elite. Convinced that the real action was happening in the "spiritual realm," we took a sharply negative view of the body and the physical world. If anything, it distracted us from what really mattered. We focused on getting more in tune with "spiritual" things, and we looked down on the "less advanced" people who hadn't reached our level of insight. We didn't care so much about feeding the hungry. We wanted to see angels and hear God.

I did hear God in the last place I expected: a philosophy class in my first term at Fuller Seminary. I learned that an "escape the body" theology has more in common with Plato than with Jesus and is at odds with the "embrace the body" theology of Scripture. That realization settled on me with great force, and I no longer could attend our prayer group. Not long afterward, the group crumbled and disbanded. I saw this as one of God's great rescue expeditions in my life and the lives of my friends. Over the years I have learned that any kind of escapist theology that pulls us away from being fully present in God's world is not worth following.

Ignore the body. While the message in the church is sometimes "escape the body," it is more often "ignore the body." We simply don't talk about it. When we do, we tend to focus on what we shouldn't do with our bodies—like "don't have premarital sex." We miss opportunities to learn about the physical nature of being a disciple of Jesus.

Like "escape the body" theology, "ignore the body" theology has more in common with our culture than with the Bible. In the modern scientific worldview, the body (and the physical world in general) is merely physical material to be manipulated and used. One's body is tissue, and it is the property of its owner. It is matter and is of a different category from spirit. The less we connect the Christian life to the body, the more natural it feels to compartmentalize our faith into "spiritual" settings like church and devotions. God gets that small sliver of activities, and we shut him out of the rest of the week. We practice God's absence because we closed the door to him when we last said "amen."

Flourish in the body. As our culture evolves, more people are looking for holistic forms of spirituality where the human person is treated as an integrated whole—physical, mental, emotional and spiritual, all together. "Escape the body" and "ignore the body" theologies are falling out of favor. Rising in their place are religiously eclectic theologies linked to practices like yoga and meditation. Rather than the assumptions that we should separate ourselves from our bodies and wait until we can escape to heaven, there is a desire to know how we can flourish as embodied persons in this world.

How will the church respond? We can offer a wealth of impactful teaching about the body, but we must know where to look.

THE BIBLE'S CONSISTENT MESSAGE

Whereas the church has sent mixed messages about the body, the Bible is clear. Rodney Clapp writes, "Classical Christian spirituality never rejects and never gives up on the body because of three key features of its basic story and logic: creation, incarnation, and resurrection."[1] To these I will add a fourth: Jesus' ascension into heaven. In embracing the physical nature of our faith, today's church is doing nothing new. We are refinding the main trail after having spent a long time wandering through brush and thickets.

Creation. Stop before you take your next breath and think about this: every breath is a gift from God. Go ahead. Breathe deeply. Step outside and take in a lungful of fresh air. Celebrate life—it's an act of worship. Even when you are asleep at night, each of those deep and restful breaths is God's gift to you. He upholds you even when you are helplessly unconscious.

The Bible tells the story of the first human breath. God gathered a lump of dust, shaped it and breathed his own breath into it. When the formed dust gasped for the first time, the man Adam was born. Adam's body was formed out of soil. You can't get more physical and down to earth than that. One day God put Adam to sleep, and he removed part of Adam's body and fashioned Eve. Now there were two human beings. God commanded them to have offspring and rule over his world. When all was finished, God looked over his creation, grounded as it was in glorious physicality and crowned with an embodied man and woman, and pronounced it "very good" (Gen 1:31).

> Walking has a way of slowing down the clock and opening our spirits. Set out on a solitary walk and start with this prayer: "Lord Jesus, how do you want to minister to me now?" Then simply open your heart and pay attention as you go. Maybe a Scripture or song will come to mind. Or you might see or hear something that sparks prayer. Take a "walk with Jesus" and be revived.

Incarnation. The word *incarnate* derives from Latin words that mean "to embody in flesh." John writes, "The Word became flesh and made his dwelling among us" (Jn 1:14). There we see it—God's embodiment (he became flesh) is coupled with God's presence (he was among us). As the apostles talked about God becoming flesh, many people found it difficult to believe. They reasoned that Jesus must be either God or human, but not both. In the face of opposition, the apostles taught that they had been with Jesus and could assure us that (a) he was a man, not a phantasm (see 1 Jn 1:1), and (b) he lived, died and rose again as only God could. He really was God in human flesh.

As a theological doctrine, the incarnation is unique. When I think about it further, it is remarkable. The Creator God fully immersed himself in the realities of his creatures. No cheating. No holding back. Jesus didn't have something up his sleeve—a secret magic that prevented him from becoming hungry, tired, grimy or smelly. In Jesus we see God as downright earthy. He knows human life from the inside and can relate to what we go through.

> *Compassion is empathizing with the plight of others and doing something to help alleviate their suffering. Compassion culminates in practical works that meet real needs. Odds are, you know someone who is suffering in some way. Do something to care for that person.*

God took on flesh for a purpose. The Bible tells us that Adam and Eve fell into sin, and humanity, the crowning masterpiece of creation, has been broken ever since. There was one way to salvage the precious wreckage: God the Son became human in order to save humans. In Jesus, God threw himself headlong into the conflict between good and evil raging on earth. The conflict was won through Jesus' physical body. On the cross, Jesus reconciled all people to God and united Jews and Gentiles (Eph 2:14-16). He achieved reconciliation in his *flesh*. The writer of Hebrews adds his own perspective. He quotes a prayer from the Greek translation of Psalm 40:6-8 and applies it to Jesus:

Sacrifices and offering you did not desire,
    but a body you prepared for me;
with burnt offerings and sin offerings
    you were not pleased.
Then I said, "Here I am—it is written about me in the scroll—
    I have come to do your will, my God." (Heb 10:5-7)

In order to save us, God got physical. It was by virtue of having a body that Jesus could do the Father's will. Unless Jesus had had a body, he couldn't have been one of us. Jesus' being one of us makes or breaks salvation. If he was, then we have a rescuer. If not, we are without hope.

Jesus wanted his followers to go into every corner of the world and make disciples. Go somewhere specifically for the purpose of spreading God's love. It could be a park or a soup kitchen, another country or your workplace. Where doesn't matter. How does. When you get there, soak up the sensations of the place. How does it look, smell, feel and sound? Who is there? Make yourself available for whatever God might want to do.

Resurrection. When I was a child, on Sundays we sometimes sang the old southern spiritual "I'll Fly Away." It begins,

Some glad morning when this life is o'er,
I'll fly away.
To a home on God's celestial shore,
I'll fly away.

I always liked the song, and now I can appreciate what it is about.

Life is wearying, and I look forward to resting with God when it is over. However, I'm no longer comfortable with the theological emphasis. What thrills me isn't "flying away." Rather, it is flourishing on an earth made new.

According to the Bible, those of us who die *will* "fly away" to be with the Lord. We will be waiting for God to bring all things to their consummation, when we can be put back in bodies where we belong. Only the new bodies won't be like the old ones. They will be imperishable and unbreakable, and we will inhabit them as whole and holy people. Our true home isn't a "celestial shore" but a remade Planet Earth that is peaceful and teeming with life. There we will thrive beyond our wildest imaginations. Our ultimate destiny is not flight from bodily existence but resurrection to a new form of bodily existence. The hope of resurrection involves being fully conformed to the good will of God, joyfully immersed in his beautiful, physical creation and finally—*finally!*—at one and in harmony with all.

Our hope is based on Jesus' resurrection. He was the first human being to be raised, and all others will eventually follow. He is our vanguard. We will eventually be raised into the same kind of body as his. According to Luke 24, the resurrected Jesus had real flesh and bones, and he could eat and drink. However, he apparently could pass through walls and doors. Jesus revealed Human Body 2.0, and he showed us that *he came to save our bodies, not just our souls.*

Ascension. Jesus' ascension into heaven is one biblical event that isn't talked about very often. Frankly, it can sound like the stuff of mythology. Jesus floated up into the sky? Really? Let's take another look at the ascension.

Luke tells us that after his resurrection, Jesus spent forty days with his followers, eating with them, instructing them and preparing them to take over his mission in the world. At the end of the forty days, Jesus blessed his friends and told them to wait in the city until the Holy Spirit was given to them. Then he rose off the ground and receded from them, ascending until a cloud obscured their view of him (Lk 24; Acts 1).

In his final departure, Jesus ascended instead of just dematerializing. It makes a statement. First, the Son's embodiment is permanent. It might be easy to view the incarnation as a short-term divine expedition: God the Son leaves heaven and goes to earth, donning human flesh while he is in the field and then quickly shedding it once he returns home. That is not the case.

Second, the Incarnate One is powerful. Jesus rose into the sky, where people understood heaven to be. The ascension was God's visual communication that Jesus was going to sit at the right hand of the Father, in fulfillment of ancient prophecy (Dan 7:13-14; Mt 26:64).

Without experiencing the ascension, Jesus' disciples would have lost a crucial part of the Jesus story. Where is he now? In the seat of power, next to the Father. What is next for him? "He will come again to judge the living and the dead" (Apostles' Creed). Jesus stayed in his skin, and this is one of the best guarantees that he will indeed return. Therefore, the salvation story relies on the ascension. Gerritt Scott Dawson writes, "Flesh is in heaven. Spirit and flesh are united. The ancient breach is healed. In Christ, we can be connected to God the Father."[2]

The alternative rock band Death Cab for Cutie had a hit song a few years ago with an opening lyric about living "where soul meets body." How do we get there? I offer three ideas from the Scriptures and the Christian tradition: surrendering our bodies, training our bodies and honoring God with our bodies.

SURRENDERING OUR BODIES TO GOD

Like so much else in the Christian life, *taking our bodies seriously starts with surrender.* In Paul's letter to the Romans, he writes at length about God's incredible mercy toward us. How can we respond? Paul's answer is shaped in a remarkably physical way: "Offer your bodies as a living sacrifice, holy and pleasing to God—this is your true and proper worship" (Rom 12:1). What a surprising twist. If I view my body as the prison house of my soul or as irrelevant to my relationship with God, I might expect Paul to say something more "spiritual." Present my *body* as a living sacrifice—obviously for Paul there is no such thing as a disembodied spirituality. What are other implications?

> Through the physical rites of baptism and Communion, God causes his grace to flow in, through and among his people. If you have committed your ultimate allegiance to Jesus but have not been baptized, then pursue baptism through your local church. If you have been baptized, make arrangements to receive Communion. Take in baptism or Communion through your senses. What are the sounds? the sights? the smells? the textures? the tastes? How does it affect you?

First, note that Paul writes "bodies" in plural but "sacrifice" in singular: "offer your bodies as a living sacrifice." If there are many bodies but one sacrifice, then our bodies make up an interconnected organism of worship. If any of us hold back, it hurts everyone else. There is no victimless sin. Ruled out are so-called private sins like cybersex, pornography, self-hatred, greed and so on. Also ruled out are self-mutilation and other acts committed against one's own body. And no, I don't think Paul would buy into the "my-body-is-my-own" defense of abortion. These so-called private acts are actually social sins committed against the rest of God's people.

Second, there is a difference between the one-time destruction of a body in an animal sacrifice and the ongoing surrender of our bodies in the way Paul is describing. This is not something we do once and are done with it. It is a daily, physical commitment of our bodies to God. This surrender of our bodies to God is, as Paul puts it, our "true and proper worship."

It is a spiritual act of worship to surrender our bodies, and all their parts, to God for his purposes. This involves asking certain questions. What do I do with my hands (used for getting things done)? my tongue (used for speaking)? my mouth (eating and drinking)? my eyes (including everything I take in visually)? my brain (thought life)? my muscles (physical activity)? my reproductive organs (sexuality)? Am I using them to serve the kingdom of God or the kingdom of self? Taking inventory of these things will probably leave us with a lot of habitual sins to confess. Confession is complete honesty with God and maybe one another. Confessing what we do with our bodies leaves us free to offer them up to God all over again, with the slate wiped clean.

TRAINING OUR BODIES ALONG WITH OUR SOULS

If it feels as if you use the parts of your body to serve the wrong purposes over and over again, don't lose hope. Clapp writes, "The body, like the soul, can be taught. It can be formed and molded. . . . The body, like a child of great potential, is too precious to be left untaught. So the formation of the whole person, body as well as soul, is at the heart of Christian spirituality."[3] Do you desire to be more godly? Your body is teachable. In the process of becoming like Jesus, "body training" is just as important as "soul training."

For help we can turn to Benedict of Nursia, founder of the Benedictine monastic movement. In Benedict's spirituality there is a blend of inner and outer elements. Inner elements revolve around *dispositions*, which include desires, intellectual convictions, priorities, experiences and intentions. The outer element of our spiritual lives is *action*, and it inherently involves the physical body.

The inner and outer elements work together. *We become what we do.* Intentional training in (inner) humility means performing (outer) humble actions constantly, over a long period of time. Personal transformation happens through thousands of minute actions in the everyday world. To take humility again, actions include praying, confessing, serving one another, listening and so on. These actions are physical and concrete. When (outer) humble actions accompany (inner) attentiveness of heart and the help of God's Spirit, God grows the virtue in our hearts little by little. We grow from prideful people who perform humble actions to humble people who are simply being ourselves. Growth is always a matter of training body and soul together.[4]

To go on a spiritual fast is to abstain from something for the purpose of drawing close to God. That something could be a necessity like food or drink, or a source of comfort like chocolate or television. The standard biblical practice is to abstain from food or drink, or both. When we fast, the physical realities are intense, but so are the spiritual benefits.

There are many ways to fast. I'll suggest one. A month after the 2010 Haiti earthquake, Haitian political leaders called a three-day fast to pray for the country. Haiti had literally been brought to its knees. We set aside the hours of 6:00 a.m. to 6:00 p.m. to abstain from food and drink as much as possible and devote ourselves to prayer, either in community or alone. Since then I have adopted the Haitian style of fasting and found that it is accessible for many people. (However, not everyone is physiologically capable of fasting from food, so please exercise care.) When I fast regularly, God does surprising things. Try fasting once a week for a month and pay attention to the spiritual effects.

The principle is, *you become what you do, so do what you want to become.* The Christian's goal is to become like Jesus. Therefore, we learn about him through the Bible, sermons and teachings. We take up actions that are like his. Living with the Holy Spirit is also key to our process. The Spirit often highlights one main thing he wants to work on at any given time. By meditating on Scripture and listening to the promptings of the Spirit, we have an ongoing divine agenda of actions custom-designed to transform us inside and out.

HONORING GOD WITH OUR BODIES

"Therefore honor God with your bodies" (1 Cor 6:20). *This is the overarching principle of a spirituality that is physical.* It happens when we surrender our bodies to God and train them for righteousness. Before elaborating on honoring God, I want to clear up one common question. How can we honor God with our bodies if the flesh is oriented toward evil?

For Paul, "flesh" is not just human skin. Dallas Willard explains,

> Those who live in terms of the "flesh"—the merely natural powers of the human being, based in the human body— have their minds set on (are totally preoccupied with) the flesh (or what they can manage on their own). He continues on to say that to have the mind "set on" the flesh in this way is "death" (Romans 8:5-6). Such a mind is naturally hostile toward God because God threatens its god. And it is unable to live in accordance with what God says, because it is working against God (Romans 8:7).[5]

The physical body is the medium by which one lives either by the flesh or the Spirit. For the Christian, Paul has incredibly lofty things to say about the physical body.

First, our bodies are sanctuaries, invested with the presence of

God. "Do you not know that your bodies are temples of the Holy Spirit, who is in you?" (1 Cor 6:19). This is an astounding truth. It is especially important if you are one of those who secretly loathes your body. God is present in every cell of your body. He created it and loves it. Right now. In your body's current condition. Without a diet or exercise program or special clothing. God has chosen your body to be his own dwelling place. What difference might it make to internalize this one theological fact?

From the weekly sabbath to the annual holidays of Passover, First Fruits, Day of Atonement and others, ancient Israel had a rich tradition of community feasts. In the spirit of celebrating what God has done, host a feast in your home for some friends. Prepare a special meal and accompany the mealtime with Scripture reading, conversation that encourages one another's hearts and a closing blessing. Make it a point to invite people you might not otherwise have over for dinner—possibly some who are outcasts. Enjoy the food, one another's fellowship and God's goodness.

Second, our bodies are the medium through which we live out our allegiances. Paul writes, "Just as you used to offer yourselves [literally, the parts of your bodies] as slaves to impurity and to ever-increasing wickedness, so now offer yourselves [the parts of your bodies] as slaves to righteousness leading to holiness" (Rom 6:19). We used to be slaves to sin, but now we have become slaves to God (Rom 6:22). We willingly hand over ownership of our bodies to our Master. Your hands, feet, limbs, torso, head—they are God's. This is a radical contradiction of Western culture's "my body is my own" dogma.

Think of the ramifications of Paul's body-embracing theology. Being great in God's eyes is not reserved for people who know secrets about the unseen realms. Far from it! Glorifying God is for all of us, and it happens in the everyday world. Wherever our bodies are, that is where the luminous glory of God can be. For some reason we don't often think of God as being deeply invested in mundane human life. The incarnation tells us otherwise. Concrete, physical, practical, everyday life is what God is all about. That is the stage on which he has chosen to demonstrate his goodness and greatness.

Prayer Exercise
Presenting Your Body

This prayer exercise could take twenty to thirty minutes and is best done sitting in a quiet place by yourself. Spend a few moments becoming still in God's presence. Then pray this prayer: "Father in heaven, in view of your great mercy toward me, I present my body as a living sacrifice." Then direct your awareness to one part of your body at a time: feet . . . hands . . . eyes . . . ears . . . mouth . . . yes, include your reproductive organs. Let no part of your body be off limits to God.

As you focus on each part, think of ways you can employ it either for sin or for righteousness. Take your hands, for instance. Will they be used for forcing your way through the world or for embracing others? Will they be industrious for your purposes or for God's? What has your history been? What do you feel God wants your future to be?

Present each part of your body to God—out loud if possible so you can hear yourself pray. At the end, adopt a physical posture of prayer—kneel down, stand, raise your hands, prostrate yourself with your face on the floor or whatever feels appropriate. Let your whole body pray. Then as you go about your day, repeat this prayer: "Father, I present my body as a living sacrifice."

BEING PRESENT
WITH ONE ANOTHER

For to us a child is born,

to us a son is given.

ISAIAH 9:6

For God so loved the world

that he gave his one and only Son.

JOHN 3:16

I PULLED MY CAR INTO THE CHURCH PARKING LOT and checked my watch. Right on time. I was leading a Bible study, and I had arrived early to pray with a couple of leaders before the meeting started. Our meetings had been marked by visitations of the peaceful and loving presence of God, and we were there to pray that he would bless us again that night. I grabbed my Bible, exited the car and walked purposefully toward the church steps. We had a half-hour before the meeting started, and I wanted to make it count.

I noticed a woman sitting on a low brick wall next to the church steps. She looked to be in her fifties and was dressed shabbily. She had a couple of large bags with her, stuffed with belongings. I didn't look too closely, but it appeared she was waiting for a ride. Assuming she didn't need me, I walked by, already entering into a prayerful state of mind.

For the next ten minutes I prayed with two of our leaders that God would meet us again that night. I looked up to see Bryan, another leader, entering the church. He came most of the way to the front, and then he turned around and went back to the front door and stopped. Standing at the open entryway to the church, Bryan was struck by an alarming contradiction. As he looked up the center aisle of the little church building, he saw three men praying about God's love. Turning to look outside, he saw a homeless woman sitting alone. He looked back at us, absorbed in our devotion to God. Turning back to the bag lady, he saw an icon of human need. Bryan couldn't live one more minute with the contradiction. He walked outside and began talking with the woman.

The next thing I knew, Bryan was walking into the church with her. *Hey, that's great,* I thought. *I love it when people in our faith community reach out.* Then I went back to praying and preparing myself for the meeting.

I failed a test that night. I believe God brought Doreen to us to see whether we would welcome her. Without even thinking about it, I had looked straight past her and excluded her from my attention. She didn't fit into my plans. The trouble was, my insensitivity to anything other than my plans ended up offending God and hurting people. God did not breathe his sweet presence into our meeting that night. It dragged, and I struggled with a sense that something was not right. Only later did I realize I had deepened a lonely woman's isolation and disappointed Bryan in the process.

That night I acted toward Doreen in ways that are entirely normal in our culture. However, there is a better way. Shining with the light of Jesus means allowing him to connect us to one another in transformational relationships.

RELATIONAL CONSUMERISM

Sin is self-determined independence from God. It is choosing to take control of our own lives rather than entrusting ourselves to God. The sin problem is worldwide, but each culture gives its own distinctive twist to relational sin. In Western culture, we come at relationships as *relational consumers,* from the standpoint of how they can benefit us. My story about Doreen is just one such story I could tell on myself.

It goes to show that even in the most pious settings—I mean, you can't get more pious than praying before a Bible study you are about to lead—we are prone to don the polished and self-important hat of the relational consumer-engineer. When we do, we become less present to God and one another. Ultimately we become lonelier people.

In the global dojo of commerce, Westerners are the black belts of consumerism. As effortlessly as a karate expert can block a punch and throw a kick, we can run through our purchasing sequence—tuning it to our desires, identifying products to fulfill our desires, choosing between products and deciding whether to purchase. Most days we run through parts of this process so many times that we don't even pay conscious attention to it. Studies show that people living in an American city are hit with as many as five thousand advertising messages in the typical day. They are everywhere. "Add this to the endangered list: blank spaces," laments *New York Times* writer Louise Story.[1] Encountering so many advertisements keeps us in consumer mode. It is ingrained habit.

When consumerism is applied to relationships, it pits investments against returns. *What do I have to put into this relationship, and what will I get out of it?* My desires are waiting to be fulfilled, and people are the products that can fulfill them. Each of us makes decisions about which people we will invest energy into. We make many of our choices based on how well people can deliver certain returns. *Is this person fun? Is he attractive? Do I gain higher social status by being with her? Can he help me make money?* And so on. The relational consumer might like and enjoy people, but in the end, consumerism is all about self. What is more, for the trained consumer it is second nature to engage people this way.

Another example would be "church shopping." Think about what is being said when we connect those two words. We are the almighty consumers, and churches and the people in them are the commodity. Church shopping can be referred to with euphemisms like "looking for a church where I can be fed," but if the motive is to have our desires fulfilled (more interesting teaching, better worship music, stronger kids' programs and so on), and we do not allow God to connect us with the church *he* wants for us, then call it whatever you want, but we are still just approaching church as consumers. We visit churches and line them up in our minds like cereal boxes on a counter. Church shopping gets whitewashed, but it is a sin as dark as any other.

Get into a prayerful state and allow God to take you through an honest tour of your relationships. Ask him where you have approached people as a relational consumer, subtly shaping your interactions with them in order to get certain returns. Then ask him where you have loved people selflessly. Confess the former and rejoice over the latter.

RELATIONAL ENGINEERING

If relational consumerism forms the self-oriented motive, relational engineering is the corresponding strategy to select and control our social circles. We construct our social lives of the best "parts" (that is, people). If someone doesn't deliver what we want, we seek to change him or her out. If I intend to better my career, I cultivate relationships with these people and stay away from those people. We call this "networking." If I wish to find a mate to make me happy, I pursue these people and exclude those people. We call this "dating." Neither professional networking nor selective dating is bad per se. It all depends on where our hearts are. Problems come when we boldly pursue our own desires, treat people like they are parts to be engineered and neglect to ask God how *he* wants to connect us to others. Relational engineering is just another way to practice God's absence.

I wish I could say the church is safe from relational engineering. While doing God's work, I have been both a perpetrator and a victim of this particular sin. I have subtly cut people out of my church circles for little more reason than that they made me uncomfortable. Shamefully, as a small group leader I once subtly pushed someone out of our group because she made me and others tense. I did this even though I have felt the sting of being excluded from the "cool circles."

When I passed by Doreen the homeless woman, my relational eyes were open to see my friends but not her. She was invisible to me, and I'm sure she knew that. If my friend Bryan hadn't brought her into our meeting that night, she would have had good reason never to darken the doorstep of another church.

Relational consumerism and engineering hurt people. You know what this feels like if you have ever been excluded because you weren't the right kind of person . . . or if you have gotten involved with others in their activities, only to find out they were using you like a pawn in a chess game . . . or if you were talking to someone at church or a party, and you could sense they were looking over your shoulder in search of someone more interesting . . . or if someone tried to change you so you would better meet their needs.

What is more, when we are the ones practicing relational consumerism and engineering, we are hurting ourselves as much as others. When we are trying to use people, we succeed only in making ourselves more lonely and destitute. Also, if we are resisting God's intention to give us away to specific people, we are cutting ourselves off from living in his life-giving presence.

> *Again, allow God to take you on a tour of your relationships. Where have you included certain people because they fit into your plans? Where have you excluded people because they didn't? What changes does God want you to make?*

GIVENNESS

There is a deeper and more beautiful way to relate to people—a way that gives life instead of draining it. We see this "better way" in the heart of our God and the story of the incarnation.

Every Christmas we celebrate the beauty of the incarnation story. And there is no more moving tribute to the Jesus story than Handel's *Messiah*, which reaches its awe-inspiring crescendo in words taken from Isaiah 9:6-7.

For unto us a child is born,
Unto us a son is given,
And the government will be on his shoulders.

And he shall be called Wonderful,
Counselor, the Mighty God,
The Everlasting Father, the Prince of Peace.

Have more lofty words ever been spoken? For that matter, has a more majestic song ever been composed? Jesus was the fulfillment of this prophetic proclamation, written hundreds of years before the first Christmas. Jesus is God's Son, given as a gift to us.

In the drama of the incarnation there are multiple players, and I want to mention the part they play in the giving of the Son. To review our trinitarian theology: we believe God exists in three persons, Father, Son and Holy Spirit. The incarnation story involves two Father-Son interactions. First, the Father *sends* the Son to save and transform the world. Second, the Father *gives* the Son as a divine gift to human beings.

The word *given* highlights the relational nature of the incarnation story. To whom was Jesus given? Usually when we Christians hear Isaiah 9:6, "To us a son is given," we assume the "us" is all of humanity. However, Jesus' givenness has three layers to it, and each is important. First, Jesus was indeed given to all of humanity. This is established not by Isaiah 9:6 but by John 3:16. In John 3, Jesus says, "For God so loved the world that he gave his one and only Son." Jesus is God's universal gift. He is the mediator between God and humanity, without whom there would be no salvation for any of us.

Second, Jesus was given to the nation of Israel. In saying "To us a son is given," Isaiah is primarily talking about Israel. The Messiah would be God's gift first to the Jews. Jesus was a light shining on the Galileans and a gift given to Israel (Is 9:1-6).

Third, Jesus was given to specific people. This is the easiest aspect of Jesus' givenness to miss. I think a lot of the time we picture Jesus as a heavenly being who was given in a nonpersonal sense to all of humanity. However, when God the Son became incarnate, he did not materialize out of nowhere with the generic title *human* stamped across his forehead. Rather, he was a particular boy, born into a particular family. He was male. He was Jewish. He lived in ancient Galilee. He had particular friends and ran around in a particular neighborhood. Later as an adult, he would connect with individual people as friends and followers.

One popular set of television commercials that began in 2007 featured "the most interesting man in the world." It is said that he once had an awkward moment, just to see how it feels. I think this is how we often picture Jesus. He must have used his powers to be the master of every situation. He always had something deep to say. He didn't mess with common pleasantries. If you said "Good morning," he would look at you with eyes that bored into your soul and reply, "How do you mean that?"

Jesus may actually have been the most interesting man in the world, but if the incarnation story is true, then he really was a man, and he navigated social life just as you and I do. He knew people not by using divine omniscience but by doing it the way we do it—getting to know them. He talked, listened, made eye contact, shared food, laughed, cried, walked and did the other things we do to build relationships. He may have even had awkward moments.

Jesus embedded himself squarely in the middle of human social life. His givenness was not a one-time thing. Day after day he allowed himself to be given away to the people around him. Some days it was familiar faces—his family and friends or his disciples. Some days it was people who would show up in a crowd. We don't see Jesus engineering his relationships to produce some worldly effect. Even in choosing his twelve disciples, he issued invitations only after spending all night in prayer (Lk 6:12-16).

Jesus' givenness highlights a couple of aspects of God's character. First, we marvel at the Son's sacrificial humility. In being given, Jesus assumed a posture of willful passivity and submitted himself completely to the will of the Father. Over many centuries of history, we human beings have demonstrated what we are all about—both miraculous love and heinous destruction. Yet to us, yes *us*, the Son allowed himself to be given.

Second, the Son's givenness points to God's highly relational nature. In being given, he throws himself into a relationship of love. We are his prize, and he is our portion. Forevermore when human beings say "us," we can include God the Son, who became one of us. *There is no more relationally rich word to describe Jesus than "given."*

PRACTICING GIVENNESS

For many years, my elderly friend Joan has been leading Bible studies for women. Not long ago a group of young women in their early twenties expressed interest in meeting with her. Joan felt she would never be able connect with them. What does a widow in her seventies have to say to women who are just beginning adult life? Joan told God she didn't think this was going to work, but if he wanted, she would give it a try. She decided simply to accept the young women and be available to them. She let herself be given away according to the Father's will. She has seen God work wonders in these relationships. She told me sheepishly, "I don't know why I ever doubted in the first place."

Being a newcomer to church or some other social circle can be a vulnerable and scary position. Make it a personal discipline to find newcomers and welcome them, no matter who they happen to be. Pay attention to them and help them feel at home.

Being given away doesn't always result in deep relationships. God can give us away for different lengths of time and various reasons. Sometimes we don't mix with people at all. Our part isn't to heap our expectations on the outcomes. It is to let God lead the process. Some outcomes are sure, however. Practicing givenness will transform your social life and your ability to be present to God in social situations. You will grow in love and prayer.

Givenness can vary, based on the context. We might encounter *moments of givenness* anywhere—running into someone in the grocery store, getting thirty seconds with a homeless person, praying with someone at church or even exchanging emails. *Short-term givenness* has a slightly longer duration. We might think of the amount of time we spend ministering to people on a short-term mission trip or interacting with extended family on a holiday vacation. Finally, there are some relationships in which we know God wants to give us to specific people for an extended period of time. *Long-term givenness* would include relationships with coworkers, roommates or friends. One relationship that should be considered permanent is marriage.

We resist being given to certain people. Often at the top of that list are immediate family members and close friends. Ongoing relationships have a way of establishing their own patterns and momentum. When my son is late for school, there are thousands of interactions that come into play. I instantly consider how often he is late for school and whether this is a pattern. If I am concerned or irritated, I jump into correctional mode, and instead of truly interacting with him, I simply try to control him.

Givenness is a disruptive force. It means that in any given moment, instead of reacting we surrender to God and ask what he wants to do. It almost always involves listening when we don't feel like it or when we think we already have the situation figured out. Nowhere is this needed more than in marriage. Many a troubled marriage could be made happy by the practice of givenness at home. Imagine a home in which each spouse surrenders to God before he or she interacts with the other. Each pays attention to the other and wants nothing more than the other's flourishing.

Other places where relational patterns set in are the workplace and church. We see the same people over and over, and our happiness in these places is often a matter of who else is there. Givenness is a game changer. Try showing up at work and church praying, "God, what do you want to do between me and these people today? How do you want to give me away?" Simply being available will open the doors to all sorts of experiences of God. Givenness further means that instead of approaching work and church as consumers who are out to find the best deal for ourselves, we allow God to keep us somewhere even if we are uncomfortable.

Pastor Dan Kimball has observed that within months of joining a church, new Christians often get sucked into the "Christian bubble" and lose their relationships with friends outside the church. We become absent from people who aren't also in the bubble. In contrast, Jesus' mission puts us squarely in the world. We can expect him to give us to people who don't yet know him.

In addition, practicing givenness prohibits us from approaching evangelism as if the next unsaved person we see were our personal project. In fact, too often in the past, evangelism has felt like relational consumerism and engineering, perpetuated by the church on unsuspecting non-Christians. In contrast, approaching non-Christians in an attitude of givenness connects us with people in humble, listening ways. Our storytelling about our lives with God arises within a context of invitation, not control.

Jesus made it a point to eat meals with people, especially "sinners." In that culture, sharing a meal communicated acceptance and unity. Try sharing a meal with someone and attaching that kind of meaning to it. At least once during the meal, make it a point to speak words of blessing over the other(s) present.

FOUR STEPS

The relational pattern Jesus sets stands in stark contrast to relational consumerism and engineering. How can we follow Jesus' pattern of givenness? How might we go from reciting "Unto us a Son is given" to saying with our hearts, *Unto others I am given?* I offer four steps to take.

Open your hands. Allowing ourselves to be given away can be scary. We don't know where it will end up. What if God wants to give me to people I don't like or trust? Can't I have my old friends? These are legitimate questions. Navigating them starts with surrendering to God.

With great honesty we acknowledge to God that there are some people who make us uncomfortable or scared or tired or stressed out, and there are other people who make us happy or fulfilled or excited. Then we prayerfully set aside our preferences and allow God to be the master of our social lives. Surrendering is a choice. It frees us to be given to whomever God chooses for whatever reason God chooses.

Prepare. Like surrendering, setting your will starts before you get into the hum of social situations. It is a decision you make in your heart. Before you interact, you decide that when you get into social situations, you will act only for the flourishing of others. It is a matter of preparation. The more prepared you are, the more of a blessing you will be to others.

Want nothing other than shalom for other people, and most of them will be glad you are around.

> *Before you enter a social interaction, whether it be at home, school, the workplace or wherever, prepare yourself with this quick prayer exercise.*
>
> *First, surrender yourself to God. You might say something like "Father, give me to others as you choose." Open your hands if you wish to feel this prayer physically.*
>
> *Second, be ready to pay attention to people by looking them in the eye and listening well.*
>
> *Third, set your will to work for the flourishing of other people. Want to see them do well in every way.*

Ask and expect. Being well prepared, we enter social interactions ready to see what God wants to do. We ask God to give us away, and we expect him to work through us. And trust me, he will. You may be surprised at whom God connects you to or for what reason. But expect God to connect you. As you are in a social situation, pay attention to how you resonate with people or where you feel a special leading to interact. Sometimes we find certain people difficult to get along with. In those cases, resonance builds only after we make an extra effort to listen carefully to someone's heart. Even the most abrasive people open up when they feel they are being listened to.

> *When you are in social settings, rather than charging ahead to interact with the people you want to talk with, take a moment to ask God if there is someone he wants you to connect with. Listen for the Father's voice and follow his lead.*

Engage people with love. Love starts with noticing people. The simple acts of looking people in the eye and listening to them are increasingly rare in our overdriven society. In refreshing contrast, showing a genuine interest in people is the starting point for Christian relationships. The difference was on display the night Doreen the homeless woman showed up outside our Bible study. I marched by her in a worldly rush, but my friend Bryan stopped to pay attention to her. Over and over, I've watched the simple act of noticing someone become the foundation on which God has done his best transformative work. Do this, and you will see radical changes in your spiritual life.

Not only did Bryan pay attention, he was focused on Doreen's well-being. He did all he could to make sure she experienced love and blessing that night. He brought her in, insisted she sit next to him, introduced her to people and prayed for her. They were simple acts, but they were intentional.

Taking a walk with someone is a great way to be present prayerfully, physically and relationally. Either out loud or in the silence of your heart, ask Jesus to walk and talk with you both, and pay attention to what you sense God doing along the way.

As we are given away in love, we place ourselves right in the middle of God's mission to save and transform through relationships. It is happening right now—quietly, almost imperceptibly, one interaction at a time. Using these minute threads, God is weaving together the fabric of his kingdom. In God's kingdom, no person is unimportant, including the Doreens of the world. No one is left unaffected. God's transforming work reaches into the hearts of those who are given as well as the recipients.

CAUTION! BEING GIVEN WILL RUIN YOUR LIFE

When we allow God to give us away, we make connections with people, and some of those connections are bound to change our lives. My friend Lucas, who introduced me and others to Haiti, likes to joke that Haiti ruins the lives of people who visit there. What he means is that the charm and charisma of the Haitians steal the hearts of Americans who visit. This is certainly what happened to me. And it happened around the theme of givenness.

The first time I went to Haiti, I was the pastoral lead on a team from our church. I was responsible for leading "brevotions" (breakfast and devotions), and I keyed in on Isaiah 9:6 and how Jesus came into this world as one who was "given to us." The theme of givenness fit perfectly for our trip. It meant asking God, "To whom do you want to give me this week? What are the *particular* connections you want to make through me?"

One afternoon toward the beginning of that trip, my daughter Lauren, who was sixteen at that time and was on our mission team, pulled me into a basketball game: two Haitian guys and me against two Haitian girls, each fourteen years old, and Lauren. Game on. I found myself guarding a strong and athletic Haitian girl named Isguerda. She spoke almost no English, and I spoke almost no Creole, but I liked her right off the bat. She was scrappy and mischievous, and she had an electric smile. At one point, just to get a rise out of her, I committed a playful foul by grabbing her arm and pulling her off balance as we positioned for a rebound. She raised her eyebrows, laughed and soon fouled me back. Communication had been established.

Little did my daughter and I know that in the midst of playing a basketball game, God had given us away. Over the course of that week, Lauren and I prayerfully decided to sponsor Isguerda and remain in relationship with her. We had no idea what that connection would mean to Isguerda. Without a father and separated from her mother, she had been begging on the streets of Port-au-Prince before being brought into the orphanage. There had been a void in Isguerda's life that God wanted to use our family to help fill.

That basketball game was in May 2009. Since then we have exchanged letters with Isguerda, and our whole family has gone to Haiti to visit her. Through several return trips, I have become a father figure in her life, and I pray for her along with my own children. I think back to the difference it made to approach that trip as people who were not there to accomplish our agenda so much as to be given away by God to someone of his choosing. God has taken that willingness and created something that shines with his beauty.

Prayer Exercise
Surrendering Our Relational Life to God.

This prayer exercise is about clearing the slate with your relationships. Get settled and center yourself in God's presence. Next, focus on situations where you played the part of the relational consumer or engineer. When have you treated someone like a product for your consumption or a part to be engineered? When have you excluded someone? Close your hands to symbolize how you have clutched, grabbed and controlled people in these interactions. Present your closed hands to the Father, openly acknowledging your sins against people and God. Now, as a gesture of releasing your past and receiving forgiveness and peace, open your hands. Present your open hands to the Father in an expression of humble gratitude. With your hands open, bring people or situations to mind in which you intend to allow the Father to give you away for his purposes. Finish this prayer time resting in the Father's wisdom and love.

THE POWER OF SURRENDER

[Christ Jesus] made himself nothing
by taking the very nature of a servant,
being made in human likeness.

PHILIPPIANS 2:7

O NE MORNING MY THEN FIVE-YEAR-OLD SON and I had a brief dispute. I asked him to brush his teeth so he could go to school. He wanted to have a debate over who is the bigger boss—his dad or the president of the United States. I thought his diversion was clever, but I could see what the real issue was. He didn't want to brush his teeth, and the president offered him a possible out. Ultimately my son wanted to be his own boss. That's what it came down to.

This little father-son moment captures a central human concern. We each answer the question *who is the boss of me?* It is the single most fundamental question of our spiritual life. Our entire existence turns on how we answer it. Sin drills into us, *I am the boss of me.* Righteousness counters, *I will let God be the boss of me, down to the smallest detail of my life.* Self-rule is the way of death and darkness. Surrender to the rule of Jesus is the way of life and light. If someone asked me, "How can I grow spiritually?" my answer would revolve around this question of who will be the boss.

We work out the "boss" question with God in two ways. Many Christians can remember a day when they formally surrendered their life to Jesus with a special prayer. I prayed that prayer when I was four years old, and it was a decisive turning point. However, one prayer does not a Jesus-follower make. From that day forward, I have encountered the "boss" question countless times. I am addressing it right now. Am I writing these paragraphs on my own, independent from God, or am I doing this as one surrendered to Jesus as Lord? In a few minutes I am going to help someone move. Then there will be emails and studying, and later on I will be coaching soccer. *How I answer the "boss" question throughout the day will make or break me as a Jesus-follower.*

AN "I AM THE BOSS OF ME" LIFESTYLE

The rock band Incubus had a hit song named "Drive." The act of driving a car became a metaphor for taking charge of one's own life. The song carries a message: don't just do what society or other people pressure you to do; instead, "hold the wheel and drive." In other words, take charge of your own choices and be yourself. Front man Brandon Boyd sings, "Lately I'm beginning to find that when I drive myself my life is found." There is a principle of psychological development here. It's hard to know who we are if we simply live by everyone else's agenda.

However, if we are talking about spirituality, "hold the wheel and drive" is a two-edged sword. On one hand, we don't want to become the dupes of a lost society by simply going with the flow. On the other hand, "holding the wheel" becomes another way of being the boss of ourselves and replaying the human tragedy of doing life without God. It feels good, but it leads to destruction.

Independence from God and self-rule are the essence of sin. This is the lesson that arises from the story of Adam and Eve. The serpent convinces Eve that she will be better off if she takes charge of her life. His plan is superior to God's. The serpent promises great rewards. He tells her what she wants to hear. Then he stands by as she takes the wheel and then convinces her husband to do the same. It's like watching two lovers drive their car off a cliff.

As the Scriptures point out, when we are the boss of us, we think we are wise and free, but we are really foolish and enslaved. We raise our arms in self-satisfied exaltation, but immediately a pair of shackles is clamped tightly around our wrists. We become slaves to our own desires and fears, and also to the "the ruler of the kingdom of the air, the spirit who is now at work in those who are disobedient" (Eph 2:2). In order to satisfy our desires and soothe our fears, we complain, manipulate, work harder, finagle, lie, seduce, network, market, fight, quarrel, lust, fantasize, demand, gossip, curse and ultimately kill.

JESUS' SELF-EMPTYING SURRENDER

Jesus had to settle the "boss question" just as we do. Would he grab the wheel and drive his own life or submit to his Father? The battle was intense, and it came quickly. Immediately after Jesus was baptized, he was led by the Holy Spirit into the wilderness to be tested by Satan. It was like a remix of the Adam and Eve story, except instead of thriving in a lush garden, Jesus was fasting in a harsh desert.

Satan offered Jesus three different ways to assert his independence from the Father. First, he could turn stones into bread in order to cut short the fast and satisfy his physical hunger. Second, he could throw himself from the top of the temple, in effect exerting control over the Father and demanding that the Father save him. Third, he could gain worldly power by bowing down to Satan, who would give him all the kingdoms of the world. Jesus overcame temptation, and in doing so he reset the human answer to the "boss question."

I picture Jesus as being a keen student of people who surrendered their lives to God. He read the prophets and identified himself as one of them (Mt 13:57; Lk 13:33). Isaiah, Jeremiah, Ezekiel—all of them chose to follow God's calling on their lives, even though they knew it would make them unpopular in many circles. Jesus followed in their footsteps.

A few years ago I read slowly through the book of Jeremiah. It took me months, but through the process I felt like I got to know the heart of the prophet. He was given a calling few would want: say hard things, knowing most people will despise both your message and you. Jeremiah wrestled with his calling, but with great clarity he prayed, "LORD, I know that people's lives are not their own; it is not for them to direct their steps" (Jer 10:23). Jeremiah's prayer rang like a bell in my heart. To this day, when marriage, parenting, work, friendships or life in general becomes difficult, and I want to be my own boss, I gain courage from Jeremiah's prayer.

Jesus was completely committed to doing the will of his Father, but he had to reach deep to remain faithful to the point of death. In the Garden of Gethsemane, Jesus asked if the Father would provide an easier way than death on a cross. Then he followed with "Yet not what I will, but what you will" (Mk 14:36-37). You can almost hear Jeremiah's voice in the background: "LORD, I know that people's lives are not their own."

These are three spiritual practices that are particularly effective in freeing us from what keeps us from being closer to God. Basic fasting is to go without food for a specific period in order to focus on more intimate contact with God. Solitude is spending a period of time away from other people. Silence is removing ourselves from conversations, email, texting and our normal intake of media. All three practices bring to the surface our attachments to things other than God, and all three clear out space for us to draw close to God. Set up a time to practice one or more of these disciplines. Even better, practice them on a regular basis (once a week, month or quarter). Let it be a time of reorganizing life under this principle: decisively cultivate what draws you closer to God and eliminate what draws you away from God.

There are two signature movements Jesus makes: self-emptying surrender (the focus of this chapter) and humble servitude (the next chapter). In Paul's churches, they celebrated these movements in worship. In his letter to the Philippians, Paul quoted the lyrics to a song his readers apparently knew. It is the oldest known Christian hymn. Paul starts with an exhortation:

> In your relationships with one another, have the same mindset as Christ Jesus.

He then quotes the song:

> Who, being in very nature God,
>   did not consider equality with God something to be used
>   to his own advantage;
> rather, he made himself nothing
>   by taking the very nature of a servant,
> being made in human likeness.

And being found in appearance as a man,
he humbled himself
by becoming obedient to death—
   even death on a cross!
Therefore God exalted him to the highest place
and gave him the name that is above every name,
that at the name of Jesus every knee should bow,
in heaven and on earth and under the earth,
and every tongue acknowledge that Jesus Christ is Lord,
   to the glory of God the Father. (Phil 2:5-11)

Embedded in the lyrics is a verb that is cryptic but packed with theological and spiritual meaning: "made himself nothing," or more literally, "*emptied* himself." The Greek verb is *kenoō*, which means to empty or drain out. In other words, although Christ Jesus was in his very nature God, he emptied himself so he could take on the nature and flesh of a member of his own creation, and humbled himself even further by becoming a slave to human beings, all of which culminated in his dying as a criminal on the cross.

The incarnation story hinges on the divine Son's self-emptying. Frankly, *without self-emptying, there is no incarnation.* And without incarnation, there is no divine light that shines in the world with unmitigated brilliance. Likewise, the Christian life hinges on our taking on "the same mindset as Christ Jesus" and undergoing our own self-emptying. *Without self-emptying, there is no following Jesus, and there is no shining with his light.*

For a short phrase, "he emptied himself" has generated a great deal of discussion in theological circles. Related to the Greek verb *kenoō* (to empty out) is the noun *kenosis* (the act of emptying). Reflecting on the Son's kenosis has been an important building block in the Christian pursuit to understand Jesus. "Kenosis theology" highlights two points about the incarnation—the act of surrender and the motive of love.

In the nineteenth century, theologians speculated at length about Jesus' kenosis. Exactly what happened to his divine powers when God the Son emptied himself? There were various answers, but they tended to unify around one central point: in order to share our human nature and live within all the conditions of human existence, except for sin, God the Son had to do without attributes like omnipotence and omniscience. That is, Jesus was one of us. He was not cheating. Nowhere is this shown more starkly than on popular Christmas cards. When we see Mary holding the infant Jesus in the stable, this is more than a sentimental moment. It represents the God of the universe, so emptied of his own privileges and powers that he is utterly helpless.

It pays to be clear about God's self-emptying. Years ago I was leading a small group discussion about the temptations of Jesus. He had been fasting in the wilderness for forty days, and he was hungry (Mt 4:2). A young woman in our group disagreed. She argued that Jesus was God and thus was above feeling hungry. In other words, the Son cheated. Several members of the group objected to the picture of a Jesus who was basically God with a human costume he could put on and take off, depending on whether he wanted to escape what was happening.

It was an important discussion, and the ramifications are far-reaching. If Jesus was cheating in the wilderness, where else was he cheating? If he did not really fast like the rest of us, then surely he would not really die on the cross, since that is a much higher degree of suffering. And if he did not die for us, then, as Paul taught, we have no hope.

Whereas nineteenth-century theologians focused on *how* the Son emptied himself, contemporary theologians prefer to talk about *why* he did it. There is less emphasis on what God emptied himself of and more on the self-emptying nature of love. Love reaches out for the other. Thus, the incarnation bursts into color as the fulfillment of God's love for humanity. He emptied himself and became one of us. He loves us that much.

The ancient song in Philippians 2:6-11 highlights the radiance of God's love. God the Son was "in very nature God." He was "adored by his Father and worshiped by the angels. He was invulnerable to pain, frustration, and embarrassment. He existed in unclouded serenity. His supremacy was total, his satisfaction complete, his blessedness perfect."[1] But the Son did not grasp and hold on to his divine privileges. Rather, he willingly laid them down for the sake of people. Grasping is not the way of God. Surrender for the sake of the other is.

This picture of God as self-emptying love is radically countercultural. The most common pictures of God swing between two extremes. On one hand, God is thought of as a self-asserting tyrant who rules with an iron fist, and people either are terrified of him or don't want anything to do with him. The tyrant God is long on power and short on compassion. He has ice in his veins. He punishes us until we capitulate to his supreme will.

On the other hand, growing in popularity is God as a cosmic nice guy. He cannot bring himself to demand anything of us beyond that each of us be a basically good person. The nice-guy God is spineless. Yet he is attractive to people because he lets you be the boss of you. Just be nice like him. And even if you aren't, he will probably not have the guts to hold you responsible. He has all the compelling excitement of cold oatmeal.

In contrast to the icy or tepid gods of pop culture, the self-emptying God of Scripture burns with a love so hot that he goes to the most outlandish extremes for the sake of the other. God emptied himself so he could become one of us and, in that face-to-face contact, call us to himself. Our picture of God shapes our lives. The tyrant God has no shortage of power-mongering imitators. The nice-guy God inspires room-temperature niceness. The self-emptying God of Scripture ushers us into a life that burns with passion and greatness.

THE BENEFITS OF SURRENDERING

In our "take charge" and "pull yourself up by your bootstraps" culture, a word like *surrender* doesn't garner much enthusiasm. "Surrender? Let someone else control your life? Why would anyone want to do that?" Actually, there is all the reason in the world to surrender. We don't simply give up our will to a fatalistic nihilism. We surrender our will to God because we trust his character. We give in, but we do so with hope. Because we are confident in God, we are also confident that "we are the winners, regardless of what we are being called upon to relinquish. God is inviting us deeper in and higher up."[2] Following are just four of the many benefits of surrendering yourself to God.

Exchange slavery for freedom. Until we surrender ourselves to God, we spend our lives being wrapped up in our own desires and fears. Richard Foster writes that surrender means freedom from the "self-sins": "self-sufficiency, self-pity, self-absorption, self-abuse, self-aggrandizement, self-castigation, self-deception, self-exaltation, self-depreciation, self-indulgence, self-hatred, and a host of others just like them."[3] It means being let out of the cramped, enclosed cell of always needing to get our own way.

Freedom from our self-imposed prison is also freedom to be in God's world in a fresh new way. Catholic theologian Thomas

Dubay says, "Only the free can love, and only the completely free can love unreservedly."[4] We can finally give to God and others our focused attention, our true companionship, our generous service, our authentic blessing, even our very selves. We discover that the air we have been breathing in the dungeon cell of our self-sins is foul and putrid. Now, liberated and out in the open, for the first time we take in a long breath of fresh air, and we finally feel truly alive.

Become more intimate with God. When we talk about surrender, we do not mean doing a few good things for God. In his book *Surrender to Love* David Benner observes that there are a lot of people who do good things for God but remain at a safe distance from him. They go through the Christian motions, but they are still their own boss.

Surrender, on the other hand, risks it all, because the question is not whether I will do something for God but whether I will *give myself* to him. There is no closer interaction we can have with God. In exchange, Jesus "welcomes us with love that invites intimacy."[5] Intimacy starts when we first realize that God accepts us. It grows as God patiently and gently opens to us first one part of ourselves and then another, and we surrender to him these previously unknown aspects of ourselves. It is like peeling back the layers of the proverbial onion. We find new intimacy with God as we surrender the increasingly tender layers of ourselves.

Hear God. The masters of the Christian tradition have consistently taught that if we want to hear God's voice, we should quiet the din of our own desires and fears. God does not often interrupt worldly conversations and pursuits. Jesus said, "Blessed are the pure in heart, for they will see God" (Mt 5:8). Purity of heart is the simplicity of loving God and weaning ourselves off what pulls us away from him.

Mother Teresa said,

An empty heart God fills. Even Almighty God will not fill a heart that is full—full of pride, bitterness, jealousy—we must give these things up. As long as we are holding these things, God cannot fill it. Silence of the *heart*, not only of the mouth—that too is necessary—but more, that silence of the mind, silence of the eyes, silence of the touch. Then you can hear him everywhere.[6]

Find meaning in life. A few years ago, my friends Chuck and Debbe were spinning their wheels at the church they were attending. They showed up for services, but their lives weren't making an impact. An inner restlessness began to mount. One day Chuck told God, "I'll do whatever you want. I just don't want to do nothing anymore." Soon after, their daughter told them there were young couples at her church who needed help. Debbe and Chuck had been married for close to forty years and had done a lot of work on their own relationship. They were excited about the idea of coaching younger husbands and wives. They started meeting with couples, and they watched God work. Today multiple marriages have been saved and strengthened through the mentoring work Debbe and Chuck have done in various living rooms around town. Their hearts have never been so full.

Finding how God wanted to use them started with Chuck and Debbe saying, in so many words, "Our lives are not our own." Surrender isn't about what we give up. It is about finding the path of true life. Margaret Silf writes that "we discover that our emptiness will lead us more surely to our true purpose than our imagined fullness ever could, because God's life and grace will flow so much more fully through empty hands."[7]

A LIFESTYLE OF SURRENDER

In a study on spiritual growth, authors Greg Hawkins and Cally Parkinson identify surrender as the number-one indicator of spiritual maturity. Less mature Christians are interested in God and active in service, but they hold on to worldly aspirations that define identity, happiness, security and success. They are still holding the wheel so they can steer their own life. The deepest spiritual growth happens when we relinquish worldly values and yield control over to Christ.[8] Below are four aspects of taking up a lifestyle of self-emptying surrender.

> *Take a few minutes to pray and prepare to listen to God. Now slowly walk through your house from room to room. Ask God to show you anything that represents an inordinate attachment in your life. For instance, your television could represent an inordinate attachment to entertainment. Whatever God shows you, take a minute to surrender that part of your life to him and ask him what he wants you to do differently. Make a plan for immediate and full obedience.*
>
> *You can also take a prayerful tour like this of your workplace, your church or any other place where your heart might have inordinate attachments.*

Prefer God and others. Recently I was experiencing difficulties with some key people in our church. I was upset, and I talked about it in my morning conversation with God. I was discouraged about being a pastor, and a big part of me wanted to find another way to make a living. Then I opened the Scriptures, and in the process of flipping from one place to another, I ran across these words of Jesus: "Whoever does not carry their cross and follow me cannot be my disciple," and "Those of you who do not give up everything you have cannot be my disciples" (Lk 14:27, 33). I felt myself facing a familiar choice: prefer myself by escaping to an easier life or prefer God by surrendering to his calling all over again.

I don't think God was saying "Suck it up and get back to work." He wanted to address my motivations. Would I ingest the soul-toxin of preferring myself at the expense of God and others? He wanted to return me to *agape* love, which looks like this: "Do nothing out of selfish ambition or vain conceit. Rather, in humility value others above yourselves, not looking to your own interests but each of you to the interests of the others" (Phil 2:3-4). Paul wrote this about human relationships, but it applies to our relationship with God as well. It should shape our approach to life. Through prayer and God's Word, we continually check our selfish ambitions and vain conceits. In humility, we prefer God and look to his interests over our own. We do the same with people. If we live like this, we will fulfill Jesus' Great Commandments to love God and neighbor (Mt 22:34-40).

Go from need to preference. A very useful tool in our spiritual life is differentiating between needs and preferences. We tend to pull various created things into the category of "need." "I need that new coat." "I need respect from my wife." "I need for you to listen to me." "I need that promotion in order for my career to stay on the right path." "I need to find my soulmate." "I need to have children." "I need . . ."

Teachers in the monastic tradition have long talked about "inordinate desires" for created things. Contemporary thinker Gerald May prefers to speak of addictions.[9] A heroin addict is convinced he needs heroin. He will do anything to get it. You may not be shooting heroin, but odds are you have become dependent on getting or experiencing certain things in life. When we are dependent, we become "users," and whatever it is we are attached to becomes our "substance of choice."

Contrast addiction and "need" language with "preference" language. "I would prefer to get that new coat." "I would prefer to receive respect from my wife." "I would prefer that you listen to me." And so on. We still feel our desires and fears, but they do not control our approach to the world around us. "I need" means I will do anything to get something, but "I prefer" means I would like it but can live without it. "I need" leads me into a dark underworld of controlling people and situations, but "I prefer" opens up sunny spaces in which I am liberated to love others entirely for their own sake.

In order to establish preference language in your heart, I suggest memorizing and meditating on Psalm 131, which contains this verse: "I have calmed and quieted myself, I am like a weaned child with its mother; like a weaned child I am content" (v. 2). In this state of surrender, we enjoy an inner stillness in which we have released all things to God. We are not clamoring for anything. *We have many preferences but no needs other than God himself.*

> *Develop an inner habit of replacing "need" language with "preference" language. Rehearse this statement: "I prefer such-and-such to be the case, but I don't need it." (For instance, "I prefer to be respected by my workmates, but I don't need it." Or "I prefer to refresh my wardrobe this year, but I don't need to.")*

Expect a battle of the will. In his book *Prayer*, Richard Foster acknowledges that relinquishing our will to God comes at the end of a pitched battle. In the Garden of Gethsemane, Jesus wept and prayed. He sweated blood. But in the end, he came to a settled state of resolve. Other biblical pillars of faith had their own battles of surrender—Abraham, Moses, David, Mary and Paul, to name a few.

We should not be surprised to find a Gethsemane experience waiting for us. Foster writes,

> The battle cry for us is "My will be done!" rather than "Thy will be done." We have excellent reasons for the banner of self-will: "Better for me than them to be in control"; "Besides, I would use the power to such good ends." But in the school of Gethsemane we learn to distrust whatever is of our own mind, thought, and will even though it is not directly sinful. Jesus shows us a more excellent way. The way of helplessness. The way of abandonment. The way of relinquishment. "My will be done" is conquered by "not my will."[10]

Receive all things as a gift. The same morning I had that humorous conversation with my younger son Nathaniel about who was the boss of him, I received a priceless gift from my older son, Spencer. He was ten at the time. I was out walking our German shepherd, Emmy, and I had chosen a route I thought would take us where Spencer would be riding his bike on his way to school.

It was a cool and still morning, and a thick fog had settled over the houses of Redondo Beach. As Emmy and I neared home, Spencer emerged out of the fog, riding toward us. At first, his face showed no recognition of who we were. I wondered if he was trying to discern whether this man and his dog posed any threat. Then, as he glided closer, a smile broke out across his face. I was expecting him to say hi as he rode by. Instead, I got something much better. He stopped, laid his bike down, and walked over and hugged me.

As Spencer pedaled off to school and Emmy and I resumed our walk, I reflected on what a gift I had been given in that simple moment. As I lifted my heart to God, brimming with joy, here's what I realized: *it is only as we surrender all things to God that we can receive all things back as gifts.* Earlier in that morning's prayer time, I had rereleased all things to God and reopened myself to whatever God wanted to give me. Having surrendered all things, I was able to receive my son with a grateful heart.

Early in the morning, before you interact with anyone else, say this prayer: "Lord Jesus, you did not clutch on to anything or anyone. I want my attitude to be the same as yours." Release each of the closest people in your life from any desire to control them. Then, as you see them, receive them as a gift from the Father. Enjoy caring for them and appreciating them from a place of freedom.

Prayer Exercise
Surrendering the Pen

God wants to write a story of revolutionary love in each of our lives. The question is whether we will let him have the pen. This prayer exercise helps us rehearse that interaction with God. Take out a sheet of paper or your journal and a pen. Get into a prayerful state in God's presence. Under one heading, list the top three things you desire most in life. Under another heading, list the top three fears you wrestle with. Ask God to help you identify these top desires and fears. Take your time and try to get to your top desires and fears, not secondary ones. After you have finished both lists, review each item, saying to God, "My will is that this desire happens" or "My will is that this fear never happens." Then go back through the list, saying for each item, "Yet for this desire or fear, not my will but your will be done." When you are finished, set down the pen in a gesture of giving yourself to God and letting him write the story of your life.

THE POWER OF HUMILITY

He humbled himself
by becoming obedient to death—
even death on a cross!

PHILIPPIANS 2:8

O NE DAY WHEN I WAS THIRTEEN, my parents gathered us three kids for a serious conversation. I had no idea how serious it would be. With tears they informed us that they were getting a divorce. The news blew up like a bomb inside me. I hadn't seen it coming, and I couldn't have been more shocked. As I considered what the future held, I was gripped with fear. Just as I was about to start high school, we kids were moving with Mom to the rough side of town.

The first day I showed up for high school, I learned that white kids were allowed to enter only through certain doors. At the apartment complex where we lived, the kids seemed to be cut from a different cloth from what I was used to. They were rougher and harder. I was overwhelmed in this new situation. My family was suddenly broken, and each of us was traumatized. We looked

around for ways to cope. The defense mechanism I found most
effective was becoming fiercely independent. I was smart and
capable, and I trusted myself more than anyone else. I went my
own way.

What I didn't know was that my defense mechanism would
become a deep and lasting spiritual problem. Since my teens,
I have been plagued by pride. I fight an ever-present impulse
to go my own way and do life without God. When I devoted
my life to Jesus as a young adult, I spent a lot of time on surrender (laying down my life) and humility (relying on God
rather than myself). I continue to focus a lot of energy on surrender and humility. I have learned that the path of Jesus is
narrow and clearly marked out. *The one and only path is surrender and humility.*

PRIDE AND HUMILITY

The tension between pride and humility isn't just my story. It is
humanity's story. The fall of Adam and Eve is marked by their
decision to find their own way to gain enlightenment rather than
relying on God. All through the Scriptures, we see this tendency
to do life without God, in both bad times and good. The story of
the exodus illustrates that when people's backs are up against the
wall—such as looking out across a barren desert and finding no
food or water—they tend to lose faith in God and rebel against
him (Ex 17:7; Ps 78:22). And Moses' last teachings, recorded in
the book of Deuteronomy, warn that when times are good and
people are comfortable, the first thing they will want to do is
forget God (Deut 8).

Israel was God's chosen nation to demonstrate to the rest of
the world that we can rely on God. But the Scriptures portray
Israel as being plagued by pride. In the period of the judges, the

most chaotic era of Israel's history, it is said that "everyone did as they saw fit" (Judg 17:6). Later the prophets railed against a culture that rejected God and stubbornly went its own way. The people are described over and over as "stiff-necked." The sages of Israel also joined the discussion. The most succinct statement about pride and humility comes from the book of Proverbs: God "mocks proud mockers but shows favor to the humble and oppressed" (3:34).

The proverb takes on even more prominence when we realize that it appears three times in the Bible—first in Proverbs 3:34 and then quoted in James 4:6 and 1 Peter 5:5. When two separate New Testament writers quote the same proverb, something significant is going on. We have hit on one of the fundamental laws of the spiritual life.

Jesus spoke about pride and humility with prophetic passion. His most famous teaching about the issue is the story of the father and his two lost sons (Lk 15:11-32). The point of the story is that pride can take more than one form, but God is happy to receive anyone who approaches him in humility. One form of pride is obvious. It is symbolized by the younger son who shames his father by demanding his inheritance early, only to go off and squander it on wild living. Picture an eighteen-year-old in Las Vegas with money to burn and no scruples. His actions say, "I don't need my father. I know well enough how to make it on my own."

Only he doesn't know how. Like Adam and Eve suffering the catastrophe of choosing their own way, the young son hits bottom in his own self-made disaster. Starving and destitute, he returns to his father in rags, a picture of newfound humility.

The wayward son's older brother illustrates a different type of pride that usually remains hidden. While his younger brother has been off disgracing the family, the older son has dutifully worked in his father's business. He does all the right things, but his heart is hard. When it comes time to show grace to his younger brother, he indignantly refuses. His inner framework is constructed of self-reliance. He openly disgraces his father by criticizing him and snubbing his request to take part in the younger son's restoration. Henri Nouwen writes, "Suddenly, there becomes glaringly visible a resentful, proud, unkind, selfish person, one that had remained deeply hidden, even though it had been growing stronger and more powerful over the years."[1]

Jesus teaches that the greatest among people will be the servant of them all (Mt 23:11). Thus, the older son would be better off bursting into the party, rejoicing wholeheartedly for his brother. Then his father could toast him and shower him with honor for being faithful and gracious. His exaltation would be magnificent. It would illustrate a principle Jesus taught: "All those who exalt themselves will be humbled, and those who humble themselves will be exalted" (Lk 14:11).

> Prayerfully think about people in your life and community. What can you do to lift up your fellow human beings? Make specific commitments and take action right away, bringing others along with you if it is appropriate. Along the way, reflect on how you are taking part in Jesus' washing the disciples' feet and saying, "I have set you an example that you should do as I have done for you" (Jn 13:15).

Pride can have a variety of faces, but it always has the same forked root: *self-reliance and self-exaltation.* Sin leads us to think too highly of ourselves and our capabilities. These are maladies known throughout human history.

Pride takes on unique forms in Western culture. Individualism revolves around self-reliance and encourages us to "pull ourselves up by our bootstraps." In the postmodern world, we distrust centralized authorities (especially the church) and instead determine for ourselves what is true and right. Each individual becomes his or her own self-exalted master. Moreover, consumerism trains us to trust in goods and services we can acquire. As consumers, we seek to elevate our station in life, and we become the masters of our own happiness.

Against my particular defense mechanisms to be self-reliant and insistent cultural training to be prideful, I have taken intentional steps to follow the one who is "gentle and humble in heart" (Mt 11:29). It has started with getting to know Jesus and how he shows what humility looks like.

JESUS' TWO GIANT LEAPS DOWNWARD

In the Christ-song in Philippians 2:6-11, God the Son empties himself and humbles himself. Self-emptying and humbling are two distinct movements, but they overlap and complement one another. We can think of self-emptying as "giving up" and humility as "taking on." First the Son gave up his divine rights and privileges. This freed him to take on human nature. Then, as a human, he humbled himself further by taking on the status of servant of all people. The message Paul drives home is that we are to imitate and join Christ in both his self-emptying and his humbling.

Let's take another look at the ancient song in Philippians 2, focusing first on verses 5-8.

> In your relationships with one another, have the same mindset as Christ Jesus:

Who, being in very nature God,
    did not consider equality with God something to be
used to his own advantage;
rather, he made himself nothing
    by taking the very nature of a servant,
    being made in human likeness.
And being found in appearance as a man,
    he humbled himself
    by becoming obedient to death —
        even death on a cross!

In 1981, when "upward mobility" was the siren call for a growing yuppie culture in the United States, Henri Nouwen wrote a series of essays in which he portrayed Jesus as paving the way of "downward mobility."[2] It is the opposite of greedy ladder climbing. It is deliberately taking a place of humility.

Downward mobility forms a powerful countercultural picture. Our culture prizes advancement and success. We admire people who climb upward and break through glass ceilings. *The way of Jesus is to descend downward and shatter glass floors.* Following the Christ-song in Philippians 2, we can think about the incarnation story as God the Son taking two giant leaps downward.

FIRST LEAP DOWNWARD: *BECOMING HUMAN*

On July 20, 1969, when astronaut Neil Armstrong stepped from the ladder of the lunar module and his left boot landed on the surface of the moon, he uttered the famous words "That's one small step for man, one giant leap for mankind." Similarly, we might say that when the newborn Jesus took his first breath, it was a big step for an infant but a giant leap for God. Whereas Armstrong's leap landed him on the moon, God's leap landed the divine Son in a food trough for farm animals.

The Son didn't take on only the parts of human nature that are convenient or easy. He was all in. The baby Jesus was as helpless as any other infant. As a boy, he developed and learned. He was sometimes tired and hungry—maybe even sick. He was socialized as a Jewish man. Like us, he needed to receive spiritual nourishment from the Father through the Spirit. God the Son had taken the leap all the way down into human nature.

To make the leap even more radical, Jesus was born into conditions that were lowly even for a human being. He entered history as a Jew living under Roman rule. Occupation forces were present, and oppression was a fact of life. Jesus' family was not well-to-do. His father was a manual laborer, and the family most likely did not own any land. I am the grandson of sharecroppers in rural Missouri, and if Jesus' life was anything like that of my mother's family, he did not have luxuries.

In the incarnation, God the Son leapt downward to the level of human beings, crashing through the barrier that separates heaven from earth and the divine from the human.

SECOND LEAP DOWNWARD: *BECOMING SERVANT OF ALL*

While God's becoming human is an enormous leap, the next one is just as shocking. The incarnate God would have been well within his rights to have walked the earth as a ruler or dignitary. But he rejected such privileges. He rejected even being equal with other human beings. Instead, he moved downward through humanity to become a servant of all people. *In the first leap downward, the Son gave up his equality with God and his divine rights. In the second, he gave up his equality with human beings and his human rights.* Two intertwined scenes from the last twenty-four hours of Jesus' life illustrate his downward leap into servanthood.

Washing the disciples' feet. Jesus interrupted the Last Supper in a most shocking way. He got up from the table, took up a basin and towel, and washed the disciples' feet one by one (Jn 13:2-5). Their culture was intensely hierarchical, and Peter's reaction tells us how baffling—even offensive—Jesus' deed was to the disciples. He saw his Master bending low to perform an action appropriate only for a slave. I picture the disciples gaping at one another in silence. Peter watched Jesus work his way slowly around the table. Matthew the former tax collector. Nathanael the truth teller. Andrew his brother. Simon the Zealot. Judas Iscariot, who minutes later would become the betrayer.

Stop and enter into that moment. What must it have been like for Jesus to wash Judas's feet?

When Jesus came to him, Peter recoiled. Maybe he pulled his feet back. "Master—*you* wash *my* feet? Never!" Jesus responded that if Peter wouldn't receive this act of humble servitude, he could no longer be Jesus' apprentice. Peter's reply is endearing: "Then, Lord, . . . not just my feet but my hands and my head as well!" (Jn 13:9).

When he finished, Jesus drove home the point.

> "Do you understand what I have done for you?" he asked them. "You call me 'Teacher' and 'Lord,' and rightly so, for that is what I am. Now that I, your Lord and Teacher, have washed your feet, you also should wash one another's feet. I have set you an example that you should do as I have done for you." (Jn 13:12-15)

Jesus did not assume the place of a slave because he was forced into it. His downward leap into servanthood was intentional. This is why Jesus was so stunningly luminous. In contrast to the darkness of a prideful world, Jesus showed his disciples a radically different way.

Submitting to crucifixion. The next morning Jesus would be hanging on a cross. His death is the ultimate symbol of Jesus' downward mobility. It is one thing for God to become a human being. It is another for God to become the servant of human beings. It is still another for God to undergo crucifixion for the sake of human beings. Crucifixion was both tortuous and degrading. It drove Jesus right through the floor of human existence. Crucifixion represented all that could be done by the powers of darkness to dehumanize God who had become human.

We recall Jesus' response to Peter at the footwashing: if Peter would not receive Jesus' act of humble servitude, he could have no part with Jesus. The same words apply to the redemption Jesus accomplished on the cross. If we want to be joined with Jesus, we have to be humble enough to receive from him. *His act of humility requires a response of humility.*

The cross shows us "how wide and long and high and deep is the love of Christ" (Eph 3:18). It is the relentless intensity of God's self-emptying love that drove him to the cross. This is a love that transcends understanding and overcomes all opponents. This is why Paul wrote to the Corinthians, "I resolved to know nothing among you except Jesus Christ and him crucified" (1 Cor 2:2). To know Christ and him crucified is to be a carrier of this intensely humble divine love.

The famous song in Philippians 2 ends with these words (vv. 9-11), reminding us that our part is to humble ourselves and God's part is to exalt. In fact, the greater the humility, the greater the honor:

Therefore God exalted him to the highest place
and gave him the name that is above every name,
that at the name of Jesus every knee should bow,
in heaven and on earth and under the earth,
and every tongue acknowledge that Jesus Christ is Lord,
    to the glory of God the Father.

GROWING IN HUMILITY

Jesus beckons us to follow him in his downward way of humility.
Nouwen stresses our need for God's help.

> The downward way is God's way, not ours. . . . We are always
> finding ourselves, even against our own best desires and
> judgments, on the familiar road of upward mobility. . . .
> Downward mobility is the diving way, the way of the cross,
> the way of Christ. It is precisely this divine way of living that
> our Lord wants to give us through his Spirit.[3]

We are called not just to appreciate humility but to grow in it.
In the following paragraphs, I will approach humility from different angles. There is not a linear way to grow in humility. It is
more like entering a forest through different access trails. The
point is not which trail we use. The point is that we keep going
deeper into the forest, spending enough time so it is not just a
place we visit but rather our home.

Truth. A big part of my personal struggle with pride has
stemmed from an improper estimation of who I am in relation to
God. Something in me is convinced that I am best off managing
life on my own. Growing in humility has meant learning and re-
learning that I need God. I am capable of leading a decent life,
but if I want to shine with Jesus' presence and do things only God
can enable me to do, I need him every day.

Nouwen recommends three key practices that can open up space for the Spirit of God to transform us into "living Christs." First, participate in the local church. *In church we hear the stories of Jesus' life, sing them, pray them in Communion and practice them toward one another. What to do: make it a discipline to attend church every week, and go in a posture of truth (knowing your own neediness) and receptivity (being ready to receive from God and serve others).*

Second, meditate on the Word of God. *We need to receive the stories of God throughout the week by reading and reflecting on the Scriptures each day in our own homes. What to do: set aside twenty to thirty minutes each day when you will read a short segment of Scripture, pay attention to the responses in your heart—whether positive or negative—and talk openly and honestly about them with God.*

Third, pray from the heart. *This is not launching a laundry list of requests toward God. It is humbly engaging God "with nothing but our own nakedness, vulnerability, and sinfulness."[4] What to do: spend ten to twenty minutes with God when you have no agenda. Talk to God with total honesty and openness about whatever is on your heart. Receive whatever he wants to say within your heart.*

Paul wrote, "Do not think of yourself more highly than you ought, but rather think of yourself with sober judgment, in accordance with the faith God has distributed to each of you" (Rom 12:3). A key to growing beyond this kind of pride is daily confession. We are plagued by sin, so we utterly depend on God to save us from destruction.

Although pride usually shows up in thinking too highly of ourselves, it can also take the opposite form. We can think too lowly of ourselves, imagining that we don't have much worth or usefulness in God's kingdom. When God wants to do something through us, we hold back. The result can be that we close ourselves off from God and choke off the flow of his grace. What can sound and look like humility ("Oh, I couldn't possibly do that") can actually be false humility. It is refusing to depend on God. Growing past this kind of pride involves owning our identity in Christ as people with an extraordinarily high calling in this world. To be humble is to rejoice over what God is doing in and through us, and live it out to the fullest.

Receptivity. One of the key moments in Jesus' story of the two lost sons is when the younger son is embraced by his father. The son has prepared a speech. He is ready to apologize to his father and propose that he be hired on as a slave. He gets out only part of his speech before his father interrupts him and calls the servants to make preparations for the son's full reinstatement. Although the son has been humbled, his humility is not complete until he stops negotiating with his father and simply receives.

Pride is trying to control God. Humility is being open and receptive toward him. As Benedictine monk William Casey puts it, humility is "a willingness to be saved, an openness to God's action, an assent to the mysterious processes by which God's plan is realized in the hearts of human beings." It is "a receptivity or passivity; a matter of being acted upon by God."[5] We know we are growing in humility when we are negotiating with God less and receiving from him more. Imagine maintaining a continual state of humble receptivity toward God throughout the day. Pursue this, and you will find happiness and peace as you discover how many ways "God shows favor to the humble."

Selflessness. In a river, a whirlpool is a spot in which everything swirls around a vacuum and eventually gets sucked into it. Similarly, a prideful person is a whirlpool for credit and attention. He manipulates situations to swirl around his voracious ego. In contrast, a humble person is willing to go unnoticed. It's not all about him all the time. He gives credit when credit is due and doesn't worry when he doesn't receive credit for himself.

It is tempting to be a whirlpool, especially in situations where we feel something important is at stake. One of my friends is up for a promotion at work, and he feels pressure to advertise his virtues to his superiors. However, God has been laying on his heart a different strategy. When asked, it is appropriate to be truthful about his strong track record, but he is to refrain from campaigning for himself. If he is going to be praised, it should come from others, not himself. With this quieter approach, he risks not getting the promotion. However, he intends to let God be responsible for the results.

Submission. For centuries, monastic leaders have designed life in their communities to be a long-term school of humility. John Cassian, an influential voice in fifth-century monasticism, relates that a new person desiring to join the monastery would not be allowed to bring in any possessions, not even a single coin, so there would be no basis for bragging or favoritism. The person would immediately be placed in submission to a superior and be required to humbly serve strangers and travelers. The monastic fathers have long known that nothing chips away at one's pride like placing oneself in submission to others.[6]

A monastic style of submission will not attract many people in contemporary Western culture. We favor treating people as equals, and we are suspicious of strict hierarchies. "Absolute power corrupts absolutely." However, wanting to flatten out the organizational structures in our society and treat everyone as equals can also be a cover for a prideful refusal to submit ourselves to another human being.

The Scriptures say, "Submit to one another out of reverence for Christ" (Eph 5:21). The fact is, *submission cultivates humility*. I don't mean blind submission that would lead you to take part in activities that dishonor God and harm people. I mean healthy submission in which you place yourself under the authority of others. Start by submitting yourself to your local church leaders.

You will not like all their decisions or theology. They are flawed people. But joyfully and patiently serving flawed leaders will both mature you and further the kingdom of God.

Servanthood. Pride is expecting others to serve our interests and agendas. Humility is elevating others above ourselves by serving them. As Nouwen puts it, "There is a profound difference between the false ambition for power and the true ambition to love and serve. It is the difference between trying to raise ourselves up and trying to lift up our fellow human beings."[7]

Elevating others by serving them is good for us. Although my wife and I have been in small group fellowships for virtually our entire adult lives, there was one season when we went without. We were busy with youth sports, school involvement and other family activities. We felt we didn't have time, so we took a break from small group. After a few months of this, I noticed a change in our family dynamics. We did a lot of good things, but most of them were oriented toward our own family. We had become like fish swimming in water that was stagnant and slowly becoming toxic. I knew what we had to do—reenter small group life so our family could serve other families. We made time for it, and the result was profound. We developed new relationships where we experienced God's love with incredible genuineness.

I recommend two additional strategies for growing by serving. First is serving people from whom we have little or nothing to gain. Jesus modeled this. He taught his followers to serve the hungry, the thirsty, the stranger, the naked, the sick and the incarcerated (Mt 25:35-36). It is good for us to take inventory of our lives from time to time. Are we serving people outside of our normal social circles at least once a month?

Second, we must serve with no strings attached. Humility means meeting someone's needs without asking for them to like us, say thank you, join our church or come to Jesus. As we take inventory of our lives, we need to ask: are we serving without asking anything in return?

Prayer. I have found that the more self-reliant I am, the less I pray. Pride and prayer don't mix well. Prayer is a struggle for me and always has been. I believe my struggles with prayer are really an indication of where my heart is. When I rely on myself, I pray less. When I rely on God, I pray more. This relationship between humility and prayer is so consistent that I have concluded there is a common spiritual law: *prayer is an indication of our humility before God.*

There is another spiritual law that follows: *if we want to grow in humility, we should work on deepening our prayer life.* There are three types of prayer that particularly help move us from pride to humility. First, we give ourselves to God and ask him to show us his plans and how he wants to involve us. This is different from asking God to bless our plans—even in prayer we can be prideful. Second, we practice confessional prayer, which humbles us. Research indicates that people who are reaching more advanced stages of spiritual maturity practice confessional prayer regularly. They are relying on God more and more. Third, we practice God's presence by connecting with him throughout the day. This kind of prayer helps me remember that I am God's creature, ut-

There are many gestures we can make with our bodies that express humility toward God in prayer. Just a few are bowing our head, kneeling, lying face-down on the floor, opening our hands receptively and lifting our arms like a child reaching up toward a father. Enter prayer now, using one or more of these gestures toward God. Pray with your body as well as your words. "Humble yourselves, therefore, under God's mighty hand, that he may lift you up in due time" (1 Pet 5:6).

terly dependent on him to supply my next breath, my next thought, my next meal and anything good in life. It helps me to walk in submission to him.

THE HAPPINESS OF HUMILITY

Michael Casey writes, "Humility brings with it a fundamental happiness."[8] We become more accepting of ourselves and others. We joyfully receive help from God and other people. We are quick to see the virtues in people rather than their faults. We serve without the insecurity that would drive us to elevate ourselves by climbing over the backs of others. We love with the freedom known only by those who give without demanding anything in return. We grow in intimacy with God because we are communing with him more and more. In short, we experience the truth of Jesus' words "Learn from me, for I am gentle and humble in heart, and you will find rest for your souls" (Mt 11:29).

Prayer Exercise
Write a Psalm to Jesus

Sit down with pen and paper or a computer, ready to pray and write. Settle yourself in God's presence and take an attitude of worship. Reread the Christ-song in Philippians 2:6-11 slowly three times. Then rewrite each verse in your own words. Choose your words carefully. Along the way, and again when you are finished, say the words to God in prayer and worship.

THE POWER OF THE SPIRIT

The Spirit of the Lord is on me . . .

LUKE 4:18

EACH ONE OF US HAS A PERSONAL HISTORY with the Spirit of God. The Spirit is the fountain of life and the source of every good thing, and none of us ever spends a moment apart from him. The Spirit is constantly working whether we notice him or not. Our personal history with the Holy Spirit is the story of how we have interacted with the movement of God in our lives.

When it comes to living in communion with the Holy Spirit, my life has wandered. The Twenty-Third Psalm means a lot to me because I feel like I have been in green pastures, beside still waters and in the valley of the shadow of death, not to mention places where I felt completely lost. Let me recount some early chapters in my personal history with the Holy Spirit.

I had the great fortune of being raised in a home where my parents practiced faith in Jesus. In fact, my father was the pastor of the First Foursquare Church of Pueblo, Colorado. Thus, my history with the Holy Spirit extends to my earliest years. My parents used to tuck us kids in at night, and we regularly said prayers. One night when I was four years old, I turned to the side and quietly invited Jesus into my heart and gave him my life. Now Jesus was not just part of the atmosphere of our home, he was the good Shepherd in my life. The Spirit was moving.

Our church was Pentecostal. I remember "words from the Lord" being frequent occurrences in church services. We occasionally had traveling revivalists visit our church, and they would preach fiery sermons and pray for the sick. I witnessed a few miraculous healings that happened in front of everyone. To me, it was entirely normal to experience the presence of the Holy Spirit in expressive worship, emotional experiences and sometimes unusual events. I learned early on that God is active and real.

At age eleven, I attended junior high winter camp along with a handful of other sixth-graders. On Saturday of that weekend, three men from the church taught a special class about the Holy Spirit. I felt like we were graduating to grownup realities. We were being ushered into the life with God that our parents were pursuing. At length and with scriptural backing, the teacher explained, "The Holy Spirit is here. He wants to fill you. He wants your life to make a greater impact. All you have to do is worship Jesus, turn away from your sins and ask for the gift of the Spirit."

The leader then asked if anyone wanted to stay for a while and pray to receive the gift of the Holy Spirit. I don't remember whether all of us raised our hands, but I did. I was aware of the gravity of the situation, and I didn't entirely know what I was getting into, but I wanted to pursue it.

As we worshiped and prayed, I was one of the last ones affected. (Of course.) I felt a wave of intense love come over me, and I started crying. I tried to hold it back—I mean, there were girls in the room. Despite my reservations, I cried anyway. And then as I kept talking to God, gradually words started coming out that I didn't know. I felt like I could control whether I allowed this other language to happen, but I couldn't control what I was saying. That was the beginning of a prayer language that has operated throughout most of my life.

I didn't know it, but my spiritual wheels were about to come flying off. Over the ensuing months, I grew more comfortable with the presence of the Spirit, and I learned about what God does in our hearts. However, when I was in eighth grade, my parents sat us kids down on the couch and gravely informed us they were getting a divorce. Not knowing what to do after that, I walked away from God. I stopped talking to God. Survival was my preoccupation. The niceties of the Holy Spirit no longer felt relevant.

During my years of high school, my mother remarried and we moved to Indiana. Throughout high school and college, I never doubted that God existed. I just didn't know what to do with him. I didn't trust him. I always felt like he was out observing my life, but he wasn't involved. However, I couldn't bring myself to sin as carelessly as many of my friends. Looking back on it, I can see the lingering presence of the Holy Spirit in my life. Even when I didn't acknowledge him, he was with me, quietly influencing me to avoid self-destructive behaviors. I partially cooperated. He was taking whatever part of my heart I would give him.

Throughout college, I tried to find my value and identity in many things: fraternity life, leadership, drinking, girls and sports. Then in my last year on campus, something unexpected happened. Intuitively I came to understand that, at the core of my heart, there was a deep and chronic ache that nothing in this world was going to cure. Somehow I knew the only answer was God. But what then? I had forgotten how to pray, let alone rely on God or live with him. Secretly, when none of my fraternity brothers were around, I started reading a Bible. I consumed the stories about Jesus with renewed interest. I began talking to God in brief and simple prayers. They were baby steps, but my life with the Holy Spirit had restarted. I didn't experience a sudden infilling of God's love and power. I just knew I was on the right track.

When I graduated, my dad offered me the opportunity to live with him temporarily in the Los Angeles area. I jumped at the chance to relocate to Southern California. Dad's invitation had one stipulation: I had to go to church with him. He was attending the Church on the Way, the flagship church of the Foursquare denomination and the home church of well-known pastor Jack Hayford. I eagerly accepted, telling Dad, "Good. That's what I want to do." I was optimistic that within the church I would re-learn how to live with God.

One night we were at a service, and Pastor Jack ended by issuing an old-fashioned altar call. He explained that there were elders at the front waiting to pray with anyone who wanted to become a Christian. Then, a couple of minutes later, he said, "I also want to invite anyone who wants to recommit your life to Jesus to come down and receive prayer." I immediately became uncomfortable. My heart was racing, and my palms started to sweat. It was as if all the lights in the room had gone out and a spotlight from heaven was focused on me. I felt glued to my chair. Yet I believed that all the prayers of the last few months had led to this moment.

Seconds slowly ticked by, and I squirmed. Pastor Jack issued his invitation a second time. I overcame my resistance, rose out of my seat and started walking. I could swear there was a half-mile of aisle between my seat and the front where the elders were standing. I was sure everyone in the church was looking at me. But with each step I cared less. I was going to do this.

When I got to the front, an older man welcomed me, and we began talking. I told him I had grown up as a Christian but had spent many years away from God. I had experienced the movements of the Holy Spirit within my soul when I was younger, but I couldn't seem to replicate those feelings. In the past I had been able to pray in another language, but now I couldn't. Was there something wrong with me? Was God reluctant to take me back?

In a word-picture, this elder spoke life-changing truth. He explained, "God hasn't left you or forsaken you. The Holy Spirit is like a river of water that used to flow through your heart. The water hasn't flowed for a long time, and the riverbed has become parched and hard. The water needs to flow for a while, and gradually the soil will become soft again. Don't worry. Just give it time and let God soften your heart." He then prayed with me, and soon I was on my way back to my seat. There were no spiritual fireworks, but I felt at peace. Over the coming weeks, everything happened exactly as the man had said. God was teaching me that my life with him is a relationship. I don't need to worry about whether he loves me, but I need to cultivate the relationship.

There are many episodes and chapters in my personal history with the Holy Spirit. Since I can't recount them all here, I will pull out the most fundamental lesson of many years of living with God. *At all times, surrendering myself to God, trusting him and depending on him have been central.* What I have entrusted to him has changed from chapter to chapter. Would I let him choose a spouse for me? As our kids have grown, would I entrust them to God? Would I trust him with our financial well-being? Would I allow him to guide my career? Would we follow him when he opened a door into pastoral ministry? How about when he asked me to be the lead pastor of a church? That was a scary one and still is. Will I let him shape, mold and use me the way he wants? That is a daily question.

Find someone who has lived a long and full life with God. Interview him or her about the Holy Spirit and some of the things God has done over the years. Write down what you learn. If possible, pray with the person you interview.

At times I have sought experiences of the Spirit as if they were the most important thing that happens between God and me. In my better times, I come to him not for what he might give me but for him alone. I worship him, surrendered to whatever he wants. Experiences of God often happen in that interaction. Another activity that frequently ushers in experiences of God is serving people. When in the midst of serving someone I feel a rush of compassion, fulfillment and happiness, I know God is present. As Mother Teresa said, "Where there is love, there is God." In short, the two occasions where I most often experience the Holy Spirit are when I love God and when I love people—in other words, when I am obeying Jesus' two core commandments (Mt 22:34-40).

Before reading on, reflect on your own history with the Holy Spirit. What are some of the key events? List them on paper. Talk to God about what they meant then and what they mean to you now. Tell someone else about them.

JESUS AND THE HOLY SPIRIT

Jesus' conception and birth. We might not often think about it, but Jesus had a personal history with the Holy Spirit. It started with Jesus' conception. The Holy Spirit came upon Mary, and she was with child (Mt 1:18). This is the story of the incarnation. As the angel Gabriel explained to Mary, the power of the Most

High would generate her pregnancy, so the child would truly be called the Son of God (Lk 1:35).

Baptism. One day when he was thirty years old, Jesus officially became the Christ. *Christ,* a Greek term, is equivalent to *Messiah,* a Hebrew term. Both mean "anointed one." This is the scene when it happened: "When all the people were being baptized, Jesus was baptized too. And as he was praying, heaven was opened and the Holy Spirit descended on him in bodily form like a dove. And a voice came from heaven: 'You are my Son, whom I love; with you I am well pleased'" (Lk 3:21-22). Whatever Jesus' interaction with God's Spirit had been before this point, at this moment he was filled with the Spirit and commissioned for his messianic mission.

Temptation. Luke goes on, "Now Jesus himself was about thirty years old when he began his ministry" (3:23). The next thing Luke reports is that Jesus was "full of the Holy Spirit" and was led by the Spirit into the wilderness (4:1). He was to be tested in the desert as the children of Israel were when they left Egypt so many generations before. But unlike the nation of Israel, Jesus would emerge from the wilderness victorious over temptation.

Ministry. Jesus had traveled south from his home in Galilee to the Jordan River to be baptized by John. He had spent forty days in the wilderness near the Jordan. Now he headed north again. "Jesus returned to Galilee in the power of the Spirit, and news about him spread through the whole countryside. He was teaching in their synagogues, and everyone praised him" (Lk 4:14-15).

After visiting several towns in the region of Galilee, Jesus returned to his hometown. Luke narrates,

> He went to Nazareth, where he had been brought up, and on the Sabbath day he went into the synagogue, as was his custom. He stood up to read, and the scroll of the prophet

Isaiah was handed to him. Unrolling it, he found the place where it is written:

"The Spirit of the Lord is on me,
    because he has anointed me
to proclaim good news to the poor.
He has sent me to proclaim freedom for the prisoners
    and recovery of sight for the blind,
to set the oppressed free,
    to proclaim the year of the Lord's favor." [Is 61:1-2]

Then he rolled up the scroll, gave it back to the attendant and sat down. The eyes of everyone in the synagogue were fastened on him. He began by saying to them, "Today this scripture is fulfilled in your hearing." (Lk 4:16-21)

Pick a day during which you are going to try to notice everything the Holy Spirit is doing in, through and around you. Where do you see God bringing about well-being and right relationships? Write down what you notice, and talk to God about it. What can you do to participate more and more in God's movements?

Jesus picked this day, in his hometown, to make important statements about who he was. A visiting rabbi was often given the privilege of expounding on the Scriptures. Jesus chose a passage that brings together his name, Jesus (Savior), and his title, Christ (Messiah). As *Savior*, Jesus would rescue people from what impoverishes, imprisons, blinds and oppresses them. As *Messiah*, he was anointed with the power of the Holy Spirit to carry out his mission. In the book of Acts, Peter would later sum up Jesus' ministry like this: "God anointed Jesus of Nazareth with the Holy

Spirit and power, and . . . he went around doing good and healing all who were under the power of the devil, because God was with him" (Acts 10:38). *When we say "Jesus Christ," we mean the Savior who was anointed with the power of the Spirit.*

Death on the cross. Jesus did not go to the cross under his own power. The writer of Hebrews explains that as he trudged up to Golgotha, stretched out his arms, was nailed to the cross and was lifted up to expire in front of the onlookers for whom he was dying, it was all done "through the eternal Spirit" (Heb 9:14). Theologian Gerald Hawthorne explains that if the Holy Spirit was extraordinarily important to Jesus all through his life and ministry, "how much more was the presence and power of the same Holy Spirit necessary at this the high water mark, the culmination, of his ministry."[1]

Resurrection from the dead. Jesus' resurrection from the dead was an act of the Trinity. In Romans 8:11, Paul teaches that the Father raised Jesus from the dead, but he did so through the Holy Spirit. The Spirit lived in Jesus and lives in us. All resurrection, both Jesus' and eventually ours, is a product of the Father acting through the Spirit.

THE SOURCE OF JESUS' POWER AND WHY IT MATTERS

When we put together the pieces, we can see that from incarnation to ministry to death to resurrection, Jesus was the quintessential person of the Spirit. His history with the Spirit highlights a crucial truth that is often overlooked: Jesus did not act autonomously. Although he sometimes talked about relying on the Father as well, there is no question that he worked with the Spirit. Matthew 12:28 is a telling verse: when asked by his critics how he was doing miracles, Jesus replied that it was by the power of the Holy Spirit. To underscore that his miracles came through the Holy Spirit, Jesus warned that to attribute the works of the Spirit

to the power of Satan is to commit a fatal blasphemy (Mt 12:31-32).
It is noteworthy that Jesus talked about his miracles as being not
his own works but the works of the Spirit.

Does it matter? Yes, and here is why. Ultimately we are ex-
ploring our ability to follow in Jesus' footsteps. If he tapped into
sources of power we don't have access to, then there is significantly less in common between Jesus and us. On the other hand,
if we have access to the same source of power that Jesus did, then
we find the common ground necessary to follow him. Klaus Issler
writes, "The degree to which Jesus depended on the Father and
the Spirit, instead of his own divine power, is the degree to which
Jesus can be our genuine example."[2]

LIVING IN THE POWER OF THE SPIRIT

We can pass off a weak facsimile of the Christian life without depending much on the Holy Spirit. We can go to church, give
money, read our Bibles and pray. Alarmingly, like Pharisees, we
can say and do the right things and still be out of fellowship with
God. Jesus showed a radically different way. The presence of the
Spirit was the fountain from which Jesus' ministry flowed, and if
we are going to live out God's mission in this world, we will draw
from the same fountain. In fact, the authentic Christian life is
impossible without the Spirit.

Living with the Spirit is possible because of a key transition in
the Trinity's work. During Jesus' ministry, the Spirit anointed him
and worked through him. After Jesus died, rose again and ascended
to the Father, the Spirit was poured out on Jesus' followers. This
crucial transition is narrated in different ways by John and Luke.
John relates that on the night before Jesus went to the cross, he
promised his disciples, "I will ask the Father, and he will give you
another advocate to help you and be with you forever—the Spirit

of truth. . . . He lives with you and will be in you" (Jn 14:16-17). Jesus fulfilled his promise by breathing the Spirit on the disciples in John 20:21-22. Luke adds detail about how Jesus' followers were filled with the Holy Spirit on the morning of Pentecost, fifty days after Jesus rose from the dead (Acts 2). Afterward God's people took up God's mission in the power of the Spirit.

In telling us about the movement of the Holy Spirit in Jesus and the early church, Luke issues an invitation. Jesus lived by the Spirit. So did the early Christians. So can we. As Jack Hayford puts it, "Imagine your heart filled with God's love, your mind filled with God's truth, your soul filled with God's life, and your body overflowing with God's goodness. That's what the promise of 'being filled with the Holy Spirit' opens to us—the invitation to be filled with God."[3]

THE "WAIT-RECEIVE-GO" PATTERN

On a typical morning, I get up before anyone else in the family. The house is quiet, and the sun has not yet risen. I make myself a cup of tea and settle into my favorite chair to spend time with God. I read from the Scriptures and other books that help draw me closer to him. I try to build a sense of leisure into that time. I want to wait on God, communing with him rather than rattling off a quick list of requests. I anticipate that he is going to say something to me, and I usually meditate on the readings and pay attention to the stirrings within my heart until I have a clear "takeaway." I talk to God about that. Then I pray for people, often taking a verse from Scripture and asking that God will bring it to bear in the lives of friends and loved ones. Before I end my time with God, I ask him to work through me during the day.

My devotions have evolved into a pattern: Wait-Receive-Go. *Wait* on God, *receive* from him, and *go* to do his mission in the world. Wait-Receive-Go is not arbitrary. It comes from the first two chapters of Acts.

Wait. Acts 1 picks up with the resurrected Jesus giving final instructions to his disciples: "Do not leave Jerusalem, but wait for the gift my Father promised, which you have heard me speak about. For John baptized with water, but in a few days you will be baptized with the Holy Spirit" (Acts 1:4-5). The disciples were chomping at the bit to see the kingdom restored to Israel. And what did Jesus tell them? "Wait."

Let me make a couple of observations from Jesus' command to wait. First, *to wait on God is to surrender.* It is to give ourselves up to God, proclaiming our need for him and wanting to see his will be done more than ours. And how does God respond? Thomas Dubay assures us, "So much does God love us that when he finds us open and ready, he cannot refrain from filling us to the extent that we are emptied."[4]

Second, *waiting on God comes before action.* This goes against the grain of our flesh. For most of us, "wait" is the most difficult instruction of all. High production and quick results hold a narcoticlike power in the Western church. Disturbingly, without waiting on God, the church's activities become an exercise in independence from God, dressed up in pious garments. In Acts 1, what had Jesus' disciples done so far? There had been no crusades,

---

How do we wait on God? We begin by showing up. Just as we wait for the bus at the bus stop, so we wait on God by putting ourselves in his presence. We are faithful in having our devotions, practicing God's presence and gathering with other believers to worship Jesus. Decide now how you are going to put yourself in God's presence in the coming month. Write it down and present your commitment to Jesus.

no initiatives, no programs, not one person rescued from human trafficking, no websites, no marketing materials, not even one Tweet. And yet Jesus put waiting before results. "Wait" was and always is Jesus' first command to his church.

Receive. Jesus promised his disciples they would receive. "Do not leave Jerusalem, but wait. . . . In a few days you will be baptized with the Holy Spirit." If waiting is a posture of self-emptying surrender, receiving is the corresponding posture of humility. We wait on our knees and receive with open hands.

Acts 1 tells us that Jesus' followers did as he instructed. They remained in Jerusalem and waited on God. Acts 2 relates that on the morning of Pentecost, as 120 of them were gathered in prayer, they received. God interrupted their prayer meeting in dramatic fashion. There was a sound like a rushing wind. There was what looked like a flame over each person's head—significantly, this included men and women, young and old. They all began speaking out about the greatness of God in languages understood not by them but by international visitors to Jerusalem who overheard them.

There are three important symbols in the Pentecost event: wind, fire and languages.

- *Wind.* Since "wind" and "spirit" are the same word in Hebrew (*ruach*), the sound of wind indicated that this was none other than the Spirit of God.

- *Flames.* The flame over each head showed them that in this new beginning of God's people, the Spirit was being given to every person equally (see Joel 2:28-29).

- *Languages.* The languages, which were heard and understood by people in the streets, pointed to Jesus' prophecy that after his followers received the Spirit, they would be his witnesses to every nation (Acts 1:8).

The symbols of the Pentecost event are important not just in the biblical story but in our lives.

- *Wind.* If we are followers of Jesus, we receive none other than the promised Holy Spirit.

- *Flames.* We receive the Spirit equally, with no regard to our age, gender, ethnicity or worldly qualifications.

- *Languages.* The Spirit fills and empowers us to live out Jesus' mission everywhere we go.

Luke includes one more important detail: the exuberant joy of the people. Outsiders thought they were drunk. We can picture a lot of hugging, laughing and at least one "I love you, man!" It probably wasn't the sound of the wind that convinced the people that the Spirit had fallen. It was that their hearts were bursting with happiness.

Pentecost reminds us that the Holy Spirit is not under our control. A good dose of receptivity, regardless of our comfort zones, would be good for us today. A mentor of mine once defined a Pentecostal as someone who wants to join with the Spirit in anything the Spirit wants to do. I replied, "Well, then I want to be a Pentecostal."

When we wait in an attitude of receptivity toward God, we should not be surprised when he gives us himself. It might look like the original Pentecost, or it might be something more like an insight or a wave of peace and love. It might happen in a religious setting like a church service or private devotions, or it might take us by surprise at a random time of the day—doing the dishes, driving the car, running or the like. Even if we have lived with God for many years, frequent infillings with his Spirit are vitally important. We cannot control what the Spirit does, but when we *wait*, we can expect to *receive* his presence however and whenever he wants to give it. *Just as God responded to an obedient, waiting, receptive church, he still responds to obedient, waiting, receptive people.*

> Pause to get into a prayerful state. Go to a faucet and turn on the water. Cup your hands to hold as much water as possible. Allow the water to run into your hands and then overflow them. Let your hands represent your soul and the water represent the Holy Spirit. Talk to the Spirit of God about how you want him to fill you up so much that he overflows and drenches the people around you.

Go. Immediately after they received the Spirit, Jesus' followers started interacting with people in the streets. When a crowd gathered, Peter preached an impassioned sermon. Thousands of people heard the message about Jesus, saw the manifestations of the Holy Spirit and wanted to know how they could become followers of Jesus too (Acts 2:37). When we are filled with the Holy Spirit, a passion for people grows within us and God's power is released through us.

Acts 2 shows us that *wait* and *receive* lead to *go*. God wants to center us in him and then turn us outward to his world. Our Spirit-empowered actions might be spectacular like Peter's sermon, but more commonly they will be small and inconspicuous, like ending an argument, saying a kind word, uttering a brief prayer or even just giving a smile. What matters is that our actions are done in the presence of the Spirit and with the aim of spreading God's love in every nook and cranny of the world.

LUMINOUS!

Jesus exuded hope. He said, "Very truly I tell you, whoever believes in me will do the works I have been doing, and they will do even greater things than these, because I am going to the Father" (Jn 14:12). Walking with the Spirit enables us to continue Jesus' work. Moreover, the Spirit makes us radiate with God's character: love, joy, peace, patience, kindness, goodness, faithfulness, gentleness and self-control (Gal 5:22-23). This is what Jesus meant when he said rivers of living water would flow from within us (Jn 7:38). That living water is the presence of God coming out in everything we do. When the Spirit is living through us, we become luminous with the brilliant presence of God.

Take some time to go through this process either alone or with others. Wait on God by reading Scripture, praying and worshiping. Place yourself at his feet and tell him you want to receive the gift of his presence. Humble yourself before him in confession and praise. Take your time and be open to when and how he might communicate himself to you. It might be a thought from Scripture, a feeling of peace or joy, a desire to serve someone, or any of many other manifestations of God's love. Be open to God and follow wherever he leads. When you conclude your time of waiting and receiving, go out in the presence of the Spirit.

Next time you go to church, try this same pattern. Wait on God as you worship and hear the Word preached. Receive his presence and message to you. Go out in the power of his Spirit to do the work he has given you to do.

PEACE

The Way That Transforms

He will be called . . . Prince of Peace.

ISAIAH 9:6

F OR THE LAST TIME I WALKED through the security doors and headed to my car. I had been working at a government aerospace facility for five years, and I had just resigned my job as a technology project manager and consultant in order to become a pastor. That final walk to my car felt surreal. I was confident I was doing what God wanted, but it was sobering to be closing the door on a corporate career path. However, my wife and I had been talking about this for a long time. I was moving into work that would put me into the thick of people's lives. There was nothing more important I could do with my life.

Many people yearn to lead lives that make a difference. A lot of Christians go to church and do religious things, but they are bored and uninspired. In *Just Courage*, Gary Haugen observes that too many Christians are traveling with Jesus but missing the adventure. Haugen writes,

In different times and in different ways, our heavenly Father offers us a simple proposition: follow me beyond what you can control, beyond where your own strength and competencies can take you, and beyond what is affirmed and risked by the crowd—and you will experience me and my power and my wisdom and my love.[1]

Abundant life is found when we give up control, follow our good Shepherd and make choices that put us in the middle of the greatest cause any of us will ever know: God's mission to make shalom.

Making shalom is the trajectory of all the previous themes of this book. Making shalom is our God-given *purpose*. It happens as we are *present*. It comes from being filled with God's *power*. Purpose, presence and power lead to making peace—a sweeping peace that changes everything.

Return to the quotation from Gary Haugen. Identify a specific issue or area in life in which Jesus is currently calling you to go where your strengths and competencies cannot take you. What do you have to risk? What about this choice might not be affirmed by the crowd? How can you follow Jesus into this adventure?

WHAT SHALOM IS

Shalom is peace—but not just any kind of peace. In popular culture, peace is usually thought of in two ways. First, we speak of peace as a feeling of tranquility. The more we are overwhelmed by suffering or the pace of our lives, the more we crave tranquility. Experiencing a "peaceful, easy feeling" is nice, but shalom is bigger than a feeling. Second, we often think of peace as a lack of conflict. To "make peace" with someone is to end hostilities. Shalom leads to the end of conflict—a time when swords are beaten into plowshares—but shalom is bigger than the absence of conflict.

According to Old Testament scholar Walter Brueggemann, shalom is *God's vision for the world*, and it encompasses every part of creation and every aspect of how we live. Shalom is how things are when God has everything the way he wants it, and there is universal harmony and wholeness. It is the complete expression of God's love for his creation.

Harmony between creatures and God. Shalom starts with how we relate to God. In the Old Testament, Israel is to be God's chosen people and host a sanctuary where the nations can find peace with God (Is 2:2-4). In the New Testament, Jesus appears as the high priest through whom all people can approach God with confidence (Heb 4:14-16). He has made peace with God for us (Rom 5:1). Shalom gained a foothold in my life when as a young adult, I ended my wanderings and recommitted myself to Jesus. Once I relearned that God's grace toward me was absolute, I could pursue relationship with him without wondering whether he accepted me.

Harmony among creatures. Shalom includes peaceful relationships throughout all of creation. Brueggemann says, "The central vision of world history in the Bible is that all of creation is one, every creature in community with every other, living in harmony and security toward the joy and well-being of every other creature."[2] Picture the lion lying down with the lamb. Picture also human beings enjoying stable and loving homes, spreading God's love around their neighborhoods, committing themselves to the public good and taking good care of God's world.

The wholeness of every creature. In shalom, not only are relationships healed but creatures themselves are made whole. Cornelius Plantinga describes shalom as *"universal flourishing, wholeness, and delight*—a rich state of affairs in which natural needs are satisfied and natural gifts fruitfully employed."[3] Revelation 21:4 tells us that in the end, when shalom is fully realized, God will wipe every tear from his people's eyes. There will be no more death or mourning or crying or pain, for the old order of things will have passed away.

Plantinga sums up well shalom's universal love and well-being. In all relationships and for all creatures, *shalom* is *how things ought to be.*

Having a vision for shalom helps us understand why sin is so disastrous. Sin is anything that disrupts shalom. In place of harmony and wholeness, sin brings oppression, violence, lust, manipulation, dishonesty, rage, theft and murder. Sin rots people, families, friendships, societies, nations, the environment and our relationship with God. This is why there is no shalom for the wicked (Is 48:22).

When we pay attention to our world, we hear an ongoing cry for shalom. I'm a music lover. No matter what genre of music I listen to, I hear singers crying out for shalom. Some songs are merely about casual sex, but most have relational themes like belonging, desire, commitment and fidelity. Like music, the themes of television shows and movies have to do with shalom and the lack of it. Beyond entertainment, social and political rhetoric holds out ideals of justice, help for the poor, peaceful international relations, environmental care and so on. Shalom is the cry of the human heart.

JESUS THE GREAT SHALOM-MAKER

God doesn't just envision shalom for us; he plans for it, accomplishes it and continually invites us into it. His shalom-making mission hinges on Jesus. In fact, the center point of God's program of shalom is the incarnation of the Son.

The story of shalom begins in the Garden of Eden. After Adam and Eve gave up the shalom of the garden and fell into sin, God promised that one day a descendant of theirs would overcome the serpent and all the evil he has introduced (Gen 3:15). Human history after the fall shows people suffering brokenness but continually reaching for harmony and wholeness.

At the right time, God sent his own Son, the Prince of Shalom, into the fray. Jesus broke open the floodgates of shalom through his pure life, sacrificial death and victorious resurrection. He was the only one who could mediate between God and humanity (Heb 12:24). As the early church fathers would argue, humanity needed salvation but could not achieve it. God could provide salvation, but he wanted it to come from within the human family. Therefore, God (who was able) became a human (who was needy).

God became fully human so he could fully save humans. Ancient church father Gregory of Nazianzus points out that Jesus redeemed whatever parts of human nature he took up. Therefore, it is vitally important that God assumed human gender, body, mind, soul, will, emotions—even human sexuality. Gregory of Nazianzus's friend Gregory of Nyssa comments that the good Shepherd "carried home on his shoulders the whole sheep, not its skin only."[4]

Jesus' new covenant was not just for the forgiveness of our sins. It was for the making of shalom throughout all of creation. "For God was pleased to have all his fullness dwell in him, and through him to reconcile to himself all things, whether things on earth or things in heaven, by making peace through his blood, shed on the cross" (Col 1:19-20).

TO MAKE SHALOM IS TO BE A CHILD OF GOD

Jesus said, "Blessed are the peacemakers, for they will be called children of God" (Mt 5:9). I must admit, this statement used to sound bland. I pictured a peacemaker as someone who would end arguments and make people feel good. Is that all Jesus wanted? My perspective changed when I understood peace as shalom. "Blessed are the shalom makers" is a statement with radical, countercultural and daring implications. I began picturing people like Mother Teresa and Martin Luther King—people who enter suffering and stand up to injustice. What is more, I understood Jesus to be implying this startling truth: *if we are not making shalom, we are not children of God.*

German theologian Jürgen Moltmann argues that the Christian life isn't just about getting saved and being nice. It is about acting as a Spirit-empowered force in the world. We should be people of hope because we look to the ultimate future when God makes all things right. That vision of ultimate shalom should inspire the way we live. We become people whose lives are given to pulling God's shalom from the future into the present. Our personal faith must impact public life.

No matter how old or young we are, where we come from or what our spiritual condition is right now, God has honored each of us with a holy commission. It is both a privilege and a responsibility to be shalom-makers in this world.

Dallas Willard teaches that growing spiritually is a combination of vision, intention and means (VIM). The same could be said for making shalom. The *vision* is shalom for the world. The *intention* is our daily decision to take up our cross and obey our calling to be shalom-makers. The *means* are many, but I will focus on three that are central: compassion, mercy and justice. To make shalom is to

- come alongside those who suffer (compassion)
- extend undeserved love (mercy)
- stand up for the oppressed (justice)

COMPASSION: *COME ALONGSIDE THOSE WHO SUFFER*

Once I attended a show by a popular rock band. In the middle of the show, the band performed a song that features the lyrics "Sheep go to heaven; goats go to hell." It is a reference to Jesus' parable of the sheep and the goats in Matthew 25. The band stayed on that line for a good two or three minutes, engaging the audience to repeat the line over and over. "Sheep go to heaven; goats go to hell. Sheep go to heaven; goats go to hell."

I grew uneasy. My church friends and I were in the midst of a pointed criticism that our culture levels at the Christian faith. It goes something like this: "The Christian God has his favorites, and he loves them like sheep, but he hates all other people and views them as goats. Christianity is judgmental and offensive. We don't want any part of it." I winced at the mocking of Jesus. And yet this is the culture we are here to reach. What to do with this critique of our faith?

The answer is in the very parable the band was quoting that night. Our culture deeply values compassion. In fact, our culture venerates people who exercise compassion and passes judgment on people who don't. With this in mind, let's turn to Matthew 25. Jesus said he will separate people the way a shepherd separates sheep from goats. On what basis? Whether they are people of compassion.

To the "sheep," the King will say,

> Come, you who are blessed by my Father; take your inheritance, the kingdom prepared for you since the creation of the world. For I was hungry and you gave me something to eat, I was thirsty and you gave me something to drink, I was a stranger and you invited me in, I needed clothes and you clothed me, I was sick and you looked after me, I was in prison and you came to visit me. . . . Truly I tell you, whatever you did for one of the least of these brothers and sisters of mine, you did for me.

In contrast, the "goats" did *not* do these things for "the least of these." Thus, they go away to eternal punishment (Mt 25:34-46).

In essence, *the sheep see people in need and do something; the goats see people in need and turn away.* Being compassionate can't save anyone, but people who belong to King Jesus are compassionate. Here a conversation with our culture opens up, since both sides elevate compassion and make it a criterion for judging people. To take it a step further, when sharing our faith, we can point people to Exodus 34:6, in which God calls himself "the compassionate and gracious God." *"Compassionate" is the first word God uses to describe himself.*

More than empathy. If compassion is so important to Jesus that he will hold us eternally responsible for it, let's be clear about what it is. In Western culture, the word *compassion* often refers to feeling sorry for people who are suffering. Empathy is good and necessary, but it is not the same as compassion. Both the sheep and the goats can feel empathy.

Without a doubt, biblical compassion *starts* with empathy. God created us to have a gut-level sense of identification with those who are suffering. The roots of the Latin word *compassio* speak of "suffering with" another. The Greek word for "compassion" in the New Testament is *splanchna,* which is a feeling arising out of one's guts. If you have wept for someone who is suffering, you know *splanchna.* Gary Haugen says that at such times "our heart is actually walking around in someone else's body."[5]

Splanchna arises in different ways. Sometimes it is as universal as saying, "He is a human being. He shouldn't have to suffer like that." Other times it is specific. "I have suffered the pain of divorce. My heart is breaking as my friends go through this." Sometimes identification requires education. As we gain insight into what others are suffering, our hearts soften toward them. The book and movie *The Help* portrays a deeply ingrained racial divide between whites and blacks in 1960s Mississippi and how it breaks down when people decide to listen to each other.

Empathy in action. Compassion is more than feeling empathy for someone who is suffering. In order for compassion to be completed, it must become *empathy in action.* In 2004 my friends Bill and Susette Manassero visited Haiti with their kids. They put on music shows at a handful of orphanages. At their final stop, they sensed something was wrong. A few months later they returned to Haiti and drove to this orphanage. As they pulled up, they saw the boys walking down the street with their meager belongings on their backs. The house had just been shut down because the proprietor had been arrested for abusing the children. Bill and Susette's hearts broke to see the boys out on the streets.

Susette and Bill prayed, "Lord, what are you going to do? You need to send someone to take care of these boys." He spoke to each of their hearts: "I have sent someone. It's you." God gave them empathy and called them to compassion. Bill and Susette responded. They hired local Haitian staff and founded Maison de Lumiere children's home. Then they sold everything and moved to Haiti. They have been there since, and Maison de Lumiere is a beacon of shalom in a formerly rough neighborhood in Port-au-Prince.

Susette and Bill had to overcome the powerful lure of the American dream. The dream is about feeling sorry for the afflicted but insulating ourselves from their suffering. In stark contrast, biblical compassion calls us not just to be aware of others' suffering but to enter into it. Compassion means living by the firefighters' motto "We run in when others run out."

If God shares his feelings with you toward someone who is suffering, the question is what he wants you to do about it. Maybe

you should pray. Or bring them a meal, send an email, go and
visit, give money or take any other number of actions that bring
about shalom. The point is not to stop at empathy. As Scripture
says, "If anyone, then, knows the good they ought to do and
doesn't do it, it is sin for them" (Jas 4:17). Not all action is helpful,
as Brian Fikkerts's book *When Helping Hurts* masterfully points
out. Still, the sheep are people of action.

MERCY: *EXTEND UNDESERVED LOVE*

When God the Son became human, it was a story not only of
compassion but also of mercy. *To show mercy is to extend God's
unconditional, reconciling love, especially when it is not deserved.*
Mercy begins with God. The writer of Hebrews explains that
Jesus had to be "fully human in every way, in order that he might
become a merciful and faithful high priest in service to God, and
that he might make atonement for the sins of the people" (2:17).
Paul also says in Romans, "While we were still sinners, . . . while
we were God's enemies, we were reconciled to him through the
death of his Son" (5:8, 10).

God's children do what their Father does. Micah 6:8 says, "And
what does the LORD require of you? To act justly and to love
mercy and to walk humbly with your God." It's not the slightly
invested "do mercy now and then" or the ever-popular "expect
other people to do mercy." It's "*love* mercy." Embrace it. Celebrate it. Sacrifice for it. Jesus said, "Blessed are the merciful" (Mt
5:7). They share in the heartbeat and movements of God.

Receive mercy. I offer three suggestions for making shalom
through mercy. First, soften your heart by taking up the discipline
of regular confession. Here is why. The more deeply we receive
God's mercy, the more we are able to give it away to others. Your
particular church tradition may have its own practices of con-

fession. I suggest this confessional prayer from the Book of Common Prayer, a prayer I have said so many times it is permanently fixed in my mind:

> Most merciful God,
> we confess that we have sinned against you
> in thought, word, and deed,
> by what we have done, and by what we have left undone.
> We have not loved you with our whole heart;
> we have not loved our neighbors as ourselves.
> We are truly sorry, and we humbly repent.
> For the sake of your Son Jesus Christ,
> have mercy on us and forgive us;
> that we may delight in your will,
> and walk in your ways,
> to the glory of your name. Amen.

Confession can be dry and formal. It can also devolve into self-condemnation. It should be renewing our humility before God, celebrating his mercy and receiving the grace to delight in his will and walk in his ways, to the glory of his name.

Show mercy. Second, we can foster mercy by becoming a non-retaliating presence. Daniel 9:9 says, "The Lord our God is merciful and forgiving, even though we have rebelled against him." Later Jesus brings it home: "Be merciful, just as your Father is merciful" (Lk 6:36). We do this by refusing to allow any offense to secure a foothold in our soul. We hold nothing against anyone. When we are mistreated—not if but *when*; when we mistreat ourselves; when we are mistreated within our family; when we are mistreated at school, at work or in our social circle; when we are mistreated in the church (sadly, some of the most grievous mistreatment happens among God's holy people)—*when* these things happen, we are to respond with mercy, refusing to perpetuate on ourselves or others even the slightest retaliation. We do not badmouth, backstab, harbor resentment or stir up criticism. We bless and do not curse (Rom 12:14) because we leave all wrath to God (Rom 12:19). It is one thing to stand up for ourselves and refuse to allow abusive situations to continue. It is another thing to retaliate and perpetuate cycles of aggression. We want to do everything we can to model mercy and thereby encourage it in others (even while not retaliating if they do not go along).

Foster mercy. Philip Yancey writes, "I rejected the church for a time because I found so little grace there."[6] Without mercy and grace, there is little room for shalom in a church. We can decide to be people of mercy by showing unmerited love to everyone who enters the church. We can do this regardless of the culture of our church, and we don't need to wait for the pastor to champion the cause. Mercy starts with the churchgoer who decides to be an agent of shalom.

JUSTICE: *STAND UP FOR THE OPPRESSED*

Compassion and justice complement one another, but they are not the same. Compassion brings us alongside those who suffer for whatever reason, whereas justice zeroes in on oppression and the use of power. *Biblical justice counters oppression by liberating victims and defending their cause.* Psalm 82:3-4 gives us the idea:

> Defend the weak and fatherless;
>   uphold the cause of the poor and the oppressed.
> Rescue the weak and the needy;
>   deliver them from the hand of the wicked.

God desires that all people have life, dignity, wholeness and the resources necessary to flourish. People with more power have the responsibility to provide these necessities for people with less power. Injustice happens when power is misused. Haugen lists some examples of injustice from Scripture:

- Cain took Abel's life through murder.

- The Egyptians took the Hebrews' freedom and dignity by enslaving them.

- King David took Uriah's wife and then Uriah's life.

- Amnon took Tamar's dignity by raping her.

- King Herod took the lives of all the boys of Bethlehem two years and younger, ordering them killed to eliminate the newborn "king of the Jews."

- The religious leaders in Jerusalem took the lives of Stephen and other believers through their civil-religious power.[7]

There are three things to notice. First, in each case, someone with more power took something from someone with less power. Second, the scale of oppression varies widely, from individual crimes to national policies. Third, the power leveraged can be of various kinds—political, societal, economic, religious, emotional or physical. Injustice is manifold. Common forms today include human trafficking, gang intimidation and crime, spousal and child abuse, genocide, global poverty, ethnic and gender-based discrimination, and abuse based on sexual orientation. Since the Scriptures tell us to "seek justice" (Is 1:17), our calling is to get involved.

Sometimes justice requires trained specialists. For instance, International Justice Mission confronts systems of slavery, sexual exploitation and other forms of violent oppression. IJM workers put themselves on the line rescuing victims, providing aftercare and prosecuting perpetrators. It is often risky work.

But ordinary people, too, can be powerful forces of justice. Not long after Sanctuary Covenant Church was planted in Sacramento, churchgoers learned of a nearby neighborhood where 567 children and youth were packed into apartment complexes on a single block. Drugs, crime and gang activity were rampant in the neighborhood. People from the church felt drawn. They started going to a park near the apartments and playing with the kids. Gradually they met the kids' families, and relationships started forming.

Volunteers began to dream of a place that could offer health, hope and renewal to this community. The small church got behind the effort, and within a year, the GreenHouse community center was founded. Over ten years, the GreenHouse has grown to provide after-school tutoring, mentoring, discipleship and leadership development. I have heard more than one kid say that if it wasn't for the GreenHouse, she or he would likely be involved in a gang. Instead, these young people are learning about God's love and thinking about junior college. The GreenHouse relies on volunteers to spend time with the kids and participate in group activities. It is an effort of ordinary people coming alongside children affected by forces beyond their control.

Every night for a week (or longer), go for a walk around your block. Pray before you go, asking God to give you eyes to see your block as he sees it. Pay attention to everything—houses/ apartments, possessions, people, living situations and so on. Where is shalom needed? What might your block be like if more shalom was happening? What is something you can do to show compassion, mercy or justice? How can you invite others on your block into making shalom for one another? Follow as Jesus leads you.

Let's say IJM or a community center like the GreenHouse isn't available to you, or you don't feel God leading you in such directions. What then? There are many ways to get involved in working for justice. One of my friends volunteers at the local juvenile hall, providing support to troubled teens. Other friends have found ways to connect with organizations fighting human trafficking in our city. The point is to get involved somewhere, and rather than throwing money at a cause, seek a way to become relationally connected.

REFRAMING EVANGELISM

Evangelism often feels like "selling Jesus" to the godless. It can make a big difference to see it as an act of compassion, mercy and justice—that is, an act of shalom. First, as compassion, evangelism is empathy in action. The great evangelists have been moved to *splanchna* by seeing so many people who don't know life in Jesus. Compassion is completed when we take action and have a conversation intended to draw someone one step closer to Jesus.

Second, evangelism is mercy. The core of shalom is our relationship with God, and evangelism is an open-hearted invitation to enjoy God's merciful, reconciling love (2 Cor 5:17-19). Evangelism is modeling and explaining the inexhaustible mercy of God.

Third, evangelism is justice because it provides liberation from spiritual oppression. Human beings are trapped in their sin, but Christ died for the ungodly and those helplessly condemned (Rom 5:6). When we participate in evangelism, we are going to those oppressed by the power of Satan (Heb 2:14) and offering them access to the One who can set them free (Lk 4:18).

MAKING SHALOM

Making shalom authentically and truthfully means doing it from a heart of love. We engage suffering, brokenness and oppression not to make a name for ourselves (as people sometimes do) but simply to bring well-being to the other. Love comes from a pure heart, and a pure heart is focused not on self but on the glory of God and the good of the person in front of us. *God is never closer than when we are absorbed in the cause of someone else.* Love also comes from a soft heart, and when we make shalom purely for the sake of the other, we find our heart turning from stone to flesh (Ezek 11:19).

Compassion, mercy and justice each address specific wrongs. What is the specific wrong that you as a shalom-maker feel called to address first? Write about a wrong that stirs your heart and captures your imagination. Answer the following questions:

- *What is a specific wrong you feel drawn to? It could be in your personal world (relationships, family, yourself), your local world (neighborhood, workplace, school, city) or the global world (international issues or the environment). (You might list a couple of other wrongs you want to address after this one.)*

- *What out of your own personal experience and makeup elicits this feeling?*

- *What images might you be able to find that express the wrong and why it matters? You might copy and paste them from the Internet or cut them out of magazines and make a collage.*

- *Finally, write out a prayer in which you pour out your heart to God about this wrong. Pray deeply. Don't hold back.*

- *If you feel God is telling you to take action, then follow his lead.*

To be a shalom-maker is to be a brother or sister of Jesus, the Prince of Shalom. Practice compassion, mercy and justice on a person-to-person level, and your life will never be dull. Be advised, though. Shalom-making is not for the faint of heart. It can be painful, costly and disruptive. But shalom-makers know there is no better way to live. "Blessed are those who hunger and thirst for righteousness, for they will be filled" (Mt 5:6). When we make shalom, the experience only makes us hunger and thirst for more.

Once you get a taste for shalom-making, your spiritual palate will be set for life. You will attest: "Blessed are the shalom-makers." What is more, you will be able to invite other people into this incredible shalom-making life. Jesus said: "You are the light of the world. . . . Let your light shine before others, that they may see your good deeds and glorify your Father in heaven" (Mt 5:14, 16). Shalom shines.

PRAYER EXERCISE: *JESUS AND RADICAL SHALOM-MAKING*

Set aside fifteen to thirty minutes, settle yourself in a quiet place, and open your Bible to Matthew 5. This prayer exercise is about entering into Jesus' showcase shalom-maker's teaching, the Sermon on the Mount.

Establish yourself in a receptive state by taking a couple of minutes to tell Jesus how much you appreciate and revere him. Talk to him about your desire to hear what he has to say.

Let's set this story in today's time. Read verses 1-2 and imagine the scene in vivid detail. Imagine Jesus sitting down on a hilltop in your hometown. What is the topography like? the weather? Who has gathered to hear him? What does the scene look and sound like? Where are you? In the story, Jesus is teaching his disciples. Are you one of the disciples? Are you someone else listening in?

Listen to Jesus' teaching. Go through the Beatitudes (vv. 3-10) once all together, and then pause to let them hang in the air for a few moments.

Go through the Beatitudes a second time, listening for how they contrast with our culture. How would Jesus' way of life be a radical shalom-making counterculture in our day?

Now go through the Beatitudes a third time, taking each one slowly. Listen for how they land in your heart. Which Beatitude above the others lifts your spirit or presents the most radical challenge to you personally? Talk with Jesus about what you hear him saying to you today and what you intend to do about it. Be specific.

Before you conclude this prayer time, read verses 13-16 about salt and light. Jesus wants us to be a radical statement of shalom in our culture. Set your will to be salty and to shine with Jesus' light. Then rest in his ability to do this in you.

CONCLUSION

High-Contrast Living

The light shines in the darkness,
and the darkness has not overcome it.

JOHN 1:5

W E TEND TO THINK OF DEEP CAVES AS STILL, silent places, but they are often alive with movement. Wind currents can create gusts up to sixty miles an hour. Water drips and flows constantly, sometimes in waterfalls that roar like jetliners. With all this, cavers report that what overwhelms one's senses more than anything else is the darkness. It is so palpably thick that caving can feel like being immersed in black ink. The most extreme cavers spend up to a month underground, and to save battery power, they turn on their lights only when performing a task that requires it. The other hours of the day they go about in the dark. The perpetual blackness plays tricks on their bodies and minds. Their sleep patterns and immune systems go haywire, and they struggle to retain their sense of direction and distance.

Prolonged immersion in absolute darkness can cause even accomplished cavers to crack.[1] When a caver's threshold for depth and darkness has been reached, it can kick off an extremely intense reaction—what author James Tabor describes as a "panic attack on steroids." Suddenly everything within the caver screams, *I've got to get out! I don't belong here!* But he or she can't get out, and this worsens the attack. Extreme cavers fear this experience and ominously call it "the Rapture." Cavers respect the darkness.

In the book of Romans, Paul portrays the spiritual state of human beings as no brighter than a cave.

> They have become filled with every kind of wickedness, evil, greed and depravity. They are full of envy, murder, strife, deceit and malice. They are gossips, slanderers, God-haters, insolent, arrogant and boastful; they invent ways of doing evil; they disobey their parents; they have no understanding, no fidelity, no love, no mercy. Although they know God's righteous decree that those who do such things deserve death, they not only continue to do these very things but also approve of those who practice them. (Rom 1:29-32)

Similarly, the apostle John describes the world as a place of spiritual darkness. Sin and evil can make it inhospitable to our souls. In fact, when we are overcome by suffering and oppression, we can have a response similar to what cavers experience, when our internal systems suddenly scream, *I don't want to be here! Get me out of this place!*

According to John, because the world had gone dark, Jesus' appearance among people was a stunning burst of light (Jn 1:5). "The true light that gives light to everyone" had come into the world (Jn 1:9). Surely John was trading on imagery used by Isaiah: "The people walking in darkness have seen a great light; on those living in the land of deep darkness a light has dawned" (Is 9:2). When God became flesh and made his appearance among us, his dazzling brilliance was like a flame deep inside a cave.

> *In the dark, a single candle can give off an explosion of light. Next time you have the opportunity, when it is nighttime, turn out the lights, bring a candle and a lighter or book of matches, and shut yourself inside a room with no windows. Sit in the darkness for five to ten minutes so your eyes become adjusted to the darkness. Then light the candle, looking as directly at it as you can. The burst of light can be so shocking that it hurts your eyes. Reflect on these words: "The light shines in the darkness, and the darkness has not overcome it" (Jn 1:5).*

Jesus not only stood out from the world, he taught us what God is like. The greater the contrast, the clearer the teaching. Think about photo editing. Without contrast, you cannot tell one part of an image from another because everything blends together. Contrast makes shapes and textures clear. Similarly, Jesus made the shapes and textures of God clear. As God among human beings, Jesus was "the radiance of God's glory and the exact representation of his being" (Heb 1:3).

A key biblical word that conveys this sense of contrast is *holiness*. Holiness is God's absolute, transcendent "otherness" from his creation. Isaiah witnessed the angels in heaven proclaiming God's majesty with the words "Holy, holy, holy is the Lord Almighty" (Is 6:3). God is often referred to in Scripture as "the Holy One." In ancient Israel there was one room in one building that was unique from all others: the holy of holies in the temple. It was the seat of God's presence and power. When Jesus came, he was the Holy One embodied (Lk 1:35). Significantly, once when Jesus cast out a demon, it screamed out, "I know who you are—the Holy One of God!" (Mk 1:24).

If you go outside in the daytime, you can look around at all sorts of things, but the sun is so intensely bright that you can't even look directly at it. God's holiness stands out from creation the way the sun stands out from all other things in our view. The more we grasp God's holiness, the more awesome it is that God passes his holiness on to us.

> Get a reference Bible and look up any six verses that talk about holiness. What do you notice? What do you want to say to God? How might God's holiness affect your daily life?

OUR CALL TO HIGH-CONTRAST LIVING

A flame in a deep cave. The sun in the sky. The incarnate God among fallen human beings. They are pictures of extreme contrast. Similarly, God has called us to high-contrast living. Jesus said, "Let your light shine before others, that they may see your good deeds and glorify your Father in heaven" (Mt 5:16). We are to stand out against our surroundings because we radiate the presence of Jesus and obey his teachings. We contend with our own sin, so we don't shine with absolute brilliance as Jesus did. However, we are to contrast to the world enough that people are drawn to God.

Even as I write these words, I feel different emotions. I am disappointed that my light doesn't point people toward God the way I'd like. Yet I don't feel mired in guilt and failure. Rather, I embrace the challenge to ascend to a higher plane in life. Shine, and by shining be a pointer that directs people to God. I want my life to be about this calling. I am willing to sacrifice for it. And I want friends around me with the same ambition so we can encourage each other. I want to see a whole community of people let their light shine and turn people toward God.

It is worth pausing to ask who we think we are. We have problems when we think too highly of our capabilities *apart from God.* This is arrogance, and our solution is humility. On the other hand, we have problems when we don't think highly enough of our capabilities *in God.* In the Scriptures, Jesus-followers are called "saints"—literally, "holy ones." We are people made holy by the death of Jesus, but having our sins forgiven isn't all that goes into the name. Saints are to shine with the holiness of God by being godly people. Our status as forgiven and our calling to high-contrast living are both captured in the term *saint.*

When we engage a life of high-contrast shining, things happen. We don't have to have our own way. We love selflessly. We make choices that contrast with the culture around us. We spend our time, talents and treasure in different ways. People start taking notice. They may not want to join us (yet), but they look on with fascination and respect. All of this leads to changes in our social lives. We establish relationships with people we would not otherwise socialize with or even meet. They might be poverty-stricken children and adults in Third World countries. Or they might be prostitutes, addicts or the homeless right in our hometown. They might include people around us who are bright and shiny on the outside but are falling apart on the inside. Once we get involved in this life, we mix with a lot more non-Christians. Living out Jesus' mission in the power of the Holy Spirit will punch a lot of holes in the so-called Christian bubble.

We also make new friends within the church. God is always relighting his church with people who make uncommon, high-contrast choices. As we join these ranks, we tend to find others who are doing the same, and we establish mutually encouraging friendships. However, there is no air of exclusivity, because we shine only through God's mercy, and we are eager for other broken people to find that same mercy.

In a high-contrast life, our relationship with God grows more intense. We encounter him not as a religious obligation but as the Lover of our soul. As we prove ourselves obedient, God entrusts us with important work. We are often stretched. We grow to love and appreciate our God of shalom much more deeply as we throw ourselves into his world in new ways. The Scriptures come alive, and our prayer life bursts into vibrant new colors. Because we are practicing God's presence, we find him eager to receive us and breathe his life into us. He is our constant provider.

On Sunday mornings, too many people are sitting in churches bored and uninspired by what they think Christianity is. In contrast, when we become people who shine, we find full and abundant life (Jn 10:10).

CHALLENGES

Just as we can be assured that we are called to enjoy all of the above blessings, so can we be assured that we will face challenges. Doing anything important in life brings us face to face with trials, conflict and failure. This is all to be expected. However, God is able to use every difficulty to work for our good and his glory.

Trials. Many spiritual breakthroughs come through trials and suffering. The light in my friends Jen and Todd has never shone brighter than after Todd's second failed bone-marrow transplant. I got to know them while Todd was in the hospital recovering from this transplant. The first time I visited him, he woke up, looked at me and told me he didn't know who I was. Just as I was about to start explaining that I was his new pastor, he informed me that he was pulling my leg. I knew I was going to like this guy.

Soon Todd came home, and over the coming weeks we all took an intense interest in the test readings that indicated whether the donor cells were taking hold. The numbers slid, and it became apparent that the second transplant was not working. Todd and Jen were devastated.

Their doctor saw some adjustments he could make, and because the donor agreed to give cells again, a third transplant was recommended. Todd and Jen agreed to it, but as they prepared for transplant day, they found themselves emotionally exhausted. They questioned whether Todd would see their daughter grow up. They wondered why God was allowing this ordeal to go on. They didn't know whether they had the inner resources to go through another transplant.

Then a curious thing happened. In the midst of uncertainties and exhaustion, they found God's peace. Together they released the entire situation to God: Todd's health, the failures of previous procedures, the success of the upcoming procedure, the future of their family—all of it. They surrendered, and God gave them rest. Not only that, but as they shared their story with others, God strengthened people around them. In the midst of suffering, they became voices who gave faith and hope to others.

Today Jen and Todd are wondering whether the third transplant is going to hold. The challenge now is to remain in the faith and hope they found at their lowest point.

Conflict. John 1:5 speaks volumes not only about Jesus but about the Christian life: "The light shines in the darkness, and the darkness has not overcome it." Shining comes with conflict. The darkness of sin and evil always moves to squelch the light of righteousness. However, Jesus gained victory over darkness and continues to reign. John tells us as much by the way he uses verb tenses in this important sentence. "The light *shines* in the darkness" (present tense), "and the darkness *has not overcome* it" (Greek aorist tense). Here the aorist tense indicates that something was completed or brought to a head. Good and evil had a fight to the death, and good won.

The light shines victoriously, but only in the midst of opposition. This is true in our lives no less than in Jesus' life. In fact, to step out into high-contrast living is to invite opposition. First, we face spiritual conflict. As disciples of Jesus, we have a personal and determined enemy. We find ourselves in the ongoing struggle between God's people and the powers of darkness (Eph 6:12).

Second, we face social resistance. When we begin standing out from the crowd, misunderstanding and criticism are not far behind. Generally speaking, people feel more comfortable when others are like them. If people are pursuing the American dream, they will want us to do the same. When we check out of the American dream, we will hear things like "You are sacrificing your career" or "Is that a safe place to take your children?" We must be prepared for this and possibly worse.

There is a story in the Gospel of Mark about a woman who took a jar of perfume worth an entire year's wages (maybe thousands of dollars worth in today's money) and poured it on Jesus' head. Others were indignant at her perceived wastefulness. "They rebuked her harshly" (Mk 14:5). But Jesus defended her and told everyone to leave her alone. "She has done a beautiful thing to me" (14:6). The story reminds us that pleasing God won't always make sense to others. Ugandan theologian Emmanuel Katongole writes,

> Mary represents the "rebel consciousness" that is essential to Jesus' gospel. Wherever the gospel is preached, we must remember that the good news will make you crazy. Jesus will put you at odds with the economic and political systems of

our world. This gospel will force you to act, interrupting the world as it is in ways that make even pious people indignant.[2]

Spiritual resistance and social resistance are different, but they have the same root: opposition to God and what he wants to do. The same darkness that tried to put out the light of Jesus is *even now* trying to put out our light. Social structures are often dominated by the values of this world. The prince of darkness, the "one who is in the world," is strong. In addition, our flesh wants to play along with the strategies of darkness. Although this is strong opposition, stronger still is the One who is within us (1 Jn 4:4). Therefore, no matter what the nature of the opposition, our solution is the same: keep our eyes not on the opposition but on Jesus, "the pioneer and perfecter of faith" (Heb 12:2).

Failure. As we set out to shine with Jesus' presence, we can expect to fail—often. My friend Amy has been a Christian most of her life, but a few months ago she felt stirred to concentrate on being the face of Jesus to the people around her. She made a prayerful commitment and set out to relate to the world in a different way. Her first stop that day was a yoga class. It was the most serene place in town, so she felt confident about maintaining her new attitude. She laid out her mat in the midst of the other students, and they began. Not long into the workout, she noticed a foot near her face. It belonged to the woman next to her. She chose to ignore it. Then a few minutes later they changed poses, and there was the foot again. She was annoyed, but she went on. Soon the foot appeared a third time, inches from her face. She took her hand and pushed the foot away. The woman lost her balance and fell over, tumbling face first into her mat. Amy felt completely defeated. If she couldn't make it through a relaxing yoga class, how was she going to do this in her high-pressure workplace?

Perseverance. The question isn't whether we will be tested by trials, opposition and failure. The question is how we will respond. James 1:2-4 gives us direction. "Consider it pure joy, my brothers and sisters, whenever you face trials of many kinds, because you know that the testing of your faith produces perseverance. Let perseverance finish its work so that you may be mature and complete, not lacking anything." There's no magic bullet or escape hatch. There is perseverance in the fellowship of Jesus and his people, who know what it's like to be tested and persevere. Perseverance in community has been key for my friend Amy, and she has found it increasingly natural to represent Jesus well everywhere from yoga class to her workplace.

Small failures are part of the process. What we want to avoid is ultimate failure—that is, not standing out at all from the world around us. *God expects high-contrast living of his people.* In Ezekiel 11:12, God sums up why he has judged the Israelites and exiled them to Babylon: "You have not followed my decrees or kept my laws but have conformed to the standards of the nations around you." The Israelites were practicing *no-contrast living* instead of the *high-contrast living* to which God called them.

Pause to think about your life. Where have trials gotten the best of you or rather served to make Jesus' light shine in you all the more? What about conflict? What about failures? Where have you persevered, and what effects have you seen from it?

PEOPLE OF GREAT SIMPLICITY

High-contrast living is not reserved for exceptional Jesus-followers. It should be normal for God's people to be the salt of the earth and the light of the world. Unfortunately, we sometimes trip over our own feet. One of my greatest challenges is overcomplicating things. One night I was at a worship gathering, and we had a special prayer time after the sermon. I was pouring out my frustrations to God because I felt my life was having no impact in his kingdom. With tears rolling down my face, I told him I felt completely clueless about what to do. I asked him to make things clear to me. I waited and prayed that way for a while. Then as I was about to give up, a picture formed in my mind of a silhouetted figure I knew to be Jesus. That was it, just Jesus. At first I thought, *That's all? Isn't there something else?* Then the message sank in. I was a systematic theologian with a propensity to overcomplicate things. God was inviting me to learn a simple way of focusing on Jesus, following him and inviting others along. I'm still learning.

Jesus himself was a lesson in simplicity. When God's people were saddled with hundreds of laws and interpretations of laws, God cut through the red tape by showing up personally. He became a man, which meant he could look people in the eye and say to them, "*I* am the light of the world. . . . *I* am the way, the truth, and the life. . . . Follow *me.*" In the end, what matters isn't whether we adhere to a religious system but rather whether we bind ourselves to the person of Jesus.

How have you overcomplicated the Christian life? When have you judged yourself or others on how well you/they adhered to a religious system rather than following closely after the person of Jesus?

Simplicity marks many of history's most luminous people. In recent times, there are two who have taught me about the power of simplicity: Billy Graham and Mother Teresa. It's embarrassing, but I remember wondering what was so special about Graham. In the mid-1980s, some friends and I went to see him speak at a rally in Anaheim Stadium. The crowd was huge, and there was an air of anticipation. We were sitting high enough in the stadium that we could both participate and observe. After worship music and other preliminary activities, Graham took the stage and delivered a straightforward message about the love of God and salvation through Jesus. As his talk unfolded, I wondered when he was going to serve up the more sophisticated "meat." His message was too simple. Then, while I grew increasingly unimpressed, he finished with an invitation to accept the grace of God through Jesus. I braced for a meager response. I felt bad for Graham, believing this message couldn't have been one of his better ones. Midway through his prayer, I opened my eyes and looked around. To my surprise, thousands of people were streaming from every part of the stadium toward the stage to begin a life with Jesus. Graham kept it simple, and God did the rest.

Mother Teresa was another public personality who could underwhelm some listeners while leaving others' hearts pounding. She spoke in a thick Albanian accent and used unadorned language, yet she exercised a gravitational pull on people. BBC reporter Malcom Muggeridge described interviewing her for a BBC television broadcast in 1968. As the cameras rolled, he asked her questions about her work in Calcutta. She delivered clear, concise responses, but they were simplistic and seemed to carry little punch. In the eyes of Muggeridge and the producers, the interview was barely usable. They considered pulling it from the broadcast, but they decided to go ahead and air it. The response astonished them. Letters, checks and money orders poured in from all over the world. People exclaimed that Mother Teresa had spoken to their hearts like no one else.[3]

Muggeridge was around Mother Teresa enough to find that it wasn't her words that captivated him and others. It was her presence. She was a bearer of something beyond herself.

She is this love in person; through her, we can reach it, and hold it, and incorporate it in ourselves. Everyone feels this. I was watching recently the faces of people as they listened to her—just ordinary people who had crowded into a school hall to hear her. Every face, young and old, simple and sophisticated, was rapt, hanging on her words; not because of the words themselves—they were ordinary enough—but because of her. Some quality that came across over and above the words held their attention. A luminosity seemed to fill the school hall, illumining the rapt faces, penetrating into every mind and heart.[4]

It wasn't only in delivering public talks that Mother Teresa shone. Muggeridge adds, "I never met anyone more memorable. Just meeting her for a fleeting moment makes an ineffaceable impression."[5] He saw people burst into tears after an interaction with her that amounted to no more than a look in the eye and a smile.

Muggeridge is of special interest because when he came to Mother Teresa, he was thoroughly dechurched and deeply cynical. He had seen the unseemly underbelly of the church and had dismissed the Christian story. It is similar to the cynicism we see today. People in our culture are quick to point out the hypocrisy, violence and moral injustices perpetuated within the Christian church. They readily dabble in world religions, but they are not quick to come to church. Notably, Muggeridge underwent a powerful and life-changing encounter with God because he saw Jesus shining through a small woman who radiated love. Mother Teresa made Jesus accessible.

Do you know anyone who is dechurched and cynical? Can you commit or recommit yourself to being a Jesus-bearer in his or her life?

Mother Teresa's luminosity came from the simple and authentic love she showed to all sorts of people, from the rich and famous to the poorest of the poor. Before she started her mission in Calcutta, she had a simple purpose: carry Jesus' presence into the "holes of the poor." She felt called to be his light among people no one else wanted. She served the poor and dying, but her first energy went to daily disciplines designed to keep her eyes on Jesus. She saw herself not as a social worker but as a Jesus-bearer. She became what the Celts describe as a "thin place"—a place where the veil between this world and heaven becomes thin and an extra measure of God's light shines through.

Shining is about having a focused life with a simple cause. I have talked in this book about purpose, presence, power and peace. I have shared many ideas and recommended dozens of practices. They all lead to this essential point: *God wants to love his world through you.* That happens by worshiping Jesus and loving the person in front of you. Do that over and over, and people will think of you as a light that shines in the darkness. But by that time you will have acquired the humility not to care much about accolades—and that will make you shine all the more.

Prayer Exercise

Read slowly through this prayer of Mother Teresa about being filled with God's Spirit and radiating his light. Go over it two or three times.

Dear Jesus, help us to spread Your fragrance everywhere
    we go.
Flood our souls with Your spirit and life.
Penetrate and possess our whole being, so utterly,

That our lives may only be a radiance of Yours.
Shine through us, and be so in us,
That every soul we come in contact with may feel Your
      presence in our soul.
Let them look up and see no longer us, but only Jesus!
Stay with us, and then we shall begin to shine as You shine;
So to shine as to be a light to others.
The light, O Jesus, will be all from You, none of it will
      be ours;
It will be You, shining on others through us.
Let us thus praise You without preaching, not by words but
      by our example,
By the catching force, the sympathetic influence of what
      we do,
The evident fullness of the love our hearts bear to You.
      Amen.[6]

What word(s) or phrase(s) jumps out at you? Talk to God about
that. Then go back and pray the whole prayer from your heart.

ACKNOWLEDGMENTS

THIS BOOK ARISES OUT OF THE TENSION between a deep-seated passion to reach for more in my relationship with God and a just-as-deep-seated tendency to get in my own way. I overcomplicate life with God, and God patiently reminds me that he wants a simple love-bond between his heart and mine. I am indebted to those who have helped me stay focused and childlike before God. There are ancient friends I know but have never met, not least among them my namesake King David and the monastic fathers and mothers. There are also contemporary friends who have spoken into my life at important times, exhorting me to keep going with God because it is the most important thing in life, and to write because they believe I have something to say. I am deeply grateful for such friends.

The first time I met IVP editor Cindy Bunch, I was convinced she had mystical powers. We met over breakfast on a Chicago morning during the great blizzard of winter 2011, called by some "Snowpocalypse." Cindy and I had been corresponding about my book project, and this was our first face-to-face meeting. Although I felt good about the basic idea, I knew something about the project wasn't quite right. For many months I had been chewing on it with a confident-but-uneasy feeling. Within five minutes, Cindy nailed the problem and laid out the solution. I leaned back in my chair and thought, *This is why great editors are priceless.* Cindy, over the ensuing months you coached and encouraged me with saintly patience. A great editor is indeed priceless. I still think you might have mystical powers.

Along the way, Cindy enlisted the help of Catherine Newhouse in trimming one of my chapters from bloated down to fighting weight. Catherine, you have no idea how much your work helped me grasp how to streamline my writing.

I salute InterVarsity Press for publishing works by small church pastors. As a small church pastor, I increasingly want to hear from thoughtful men and women who are leading churches of a couple hundred people or less. Those voices are important to the health of the church in the postmodern world. And speaking of InterVarsity, I want to thank Christie Heller de Leon for connecting me to IVP in the first place.

I am deeply grateful to the people who have prayed for me while I worked on this project. You know you are. More important, God knows who you are. I pray all his richest rewards for you. Greg Krieger, Scott Buetzow and Bret Widman—we share the journey. You carry me when I falter and rejoice with me when I flourish. John Wright, my conversations with you helped me connect and reconnect with a passion for God. Larry Eissler, you are one of a kind, and I thank you for your encouragement every step of the way. Sylvia Wagner, your support is so extensive that without you in our lives, I'm not sure this book would have happened.

I have written this book as a working pastor of a beautiful faith community. I thank the people of Sanctuary Covenant Church in Sacramento for encouraging me to write. I love this church! Thanks to Brian, Elize, Chuck, Debbe, Dawnelle, Judy, Kyle,

Jana, Jason, Matt, Laurie, Ann and others who participated in discussions of earlier (i.e., bloated) drafts of the material. I want to thank Amy for providing me with my favorite story in the whole book, the "yoga story." I also thank you for helping me think about how to put this book into as many hands as possible.

David Meinke and Sean Curtis, thank you for providing specific feedback on particular chapters. Tim Morey, we have now been readers for each other's books, and I couldn't be happier! I appreciate you a great deal, my friend.

And now to family. I thank my dad and mom for passing down the zeal to know and experience Jesus here and now. That is the kernel of this book. You each fed into this book in your own ways. Thanks to Jerry, Dabney and Jon for your encouragement to keep going. Diane, no one had a more important hand in bringing this book to its finished state than you did. You are brilliant, and you're in my corner. How fortunate I am!

My kids, Lauren, Spencer and Nathaniel, all celebrated milestones of the book's development, gave me space to write and cheered me on. Kids, each of you is "luminous" in your own unique way! Isguerda, you have the smile that lights up every room. Finally, I want to thank my wife, Susan. I have seen you shine with Jesus' presence as you love and serve people, especially those in need of a good listener and compassionate heart. One word from you and I am ready to climb a mountain. You make me want to be better.

Appendix 1

SEE THE LIGHT

Questions for Discussion and Reflection

Following are questions to stir reflection and lead to deeper personal understanding. You can work through these questions by yourself or with a few other people.

CHAPTER 1: SHINING LIKE STARS

1. Malcolm Muggeridge believed God wants to manifest himself through us similarly to how he did through Jesus. To what extent would you agree or disagree with Muggeridge?

2. Do you know anyone who shines with the presence of Jesus? What about them is luminescent? What qualities do they reveal about God?

3. What are the three primary meanings of the word *shine* as it is used in Scripture? How does Jesus shine in these three ways?

4. If you were to pray the biblical prayer that God would shine in the world around you, what would you be asking him to do? How might you incorporate this prayer into your daily conversation with God? Where would you like him to shine first and foremost?

5. What would it mean for God to shine through you? What is one way you are squelching the light, and how would you like to see it be brighter?

6. What is the difference between "seeing the light," "following the light" and "shining with the light"? How are they inter-related? Why shouldn't we settle for "seeing the light"?

CHAPTER 2: PURPOSE: *KNOWING WHY WE ARE HERE*

1. What are the one or two most stirring insights you received while reading this chapter?

2. Can you remember a time when you were sent by someone else on a specific mission? It could be something small like a trip to the grocery store or something big like serving in the armed services or something in between. Reflect on that experience. What difference did it make that you were "sent"?

3. To what extent would you agree that many Christians seem to want to mix God's purposes in with their own purposes? What would happen if more Christians lived with only one ultimate purpose? Take an honest look at your big choices over the last three years. Do they reflect double (or multiple) allegiances or a single allegiance to Jesus? Do they reflect growth in allegiance to Jesus or stagnation or even falling away?

4. What do you think of all those instances in the Gospel of John when Jesus referred to himself as being sent by the Father? How does knowing this about Jesus affect the way you understand him and follow him?

5. Think about salvation in holistic terms. God not only wants to forgive our guilt and invite us into heaven, he also wants everything within us and throughout the world to be "the way it ought to be." How does this expansive idea of salvation affect the way you "work out your salvation" (Phil 2:12)?

6. Of the five ways to grow in your sense of being sent, where do you feel most compelled to start working today? What is a commitment you can make toward your own growth?

CHAPTER 3: BEING PRESENT WITH GOD

1. Talk about the remote and absent God of Western thought. Where have you encountered this kind of theology? Think about what is said and acted out in school, politics, sports, social settings, your neighborhood and other places. How does the story of God's absence get acted out around you?

2. To what extent do you buy into a theology of God's absence by practicing God's absence? How do you feel about the prospect of being connected with God's presence throughout the day?

3. Explain the story of the incarnation in your own words, focusing particularly on the theme of Immanuel, God being present with us in the person of Jesus. In what ways does Jesus' being Immanuel change human history?

4. Try this exercise with a group or a conversation partner. With your partner(s) in one room, exit to a place where you are out of sight. Loudly from the other room, read these verses: "Hear, O Israel: The LORD our God, the LORD is one. Love the LORD your God with all your heart and with all your soul and with all your strength" (Deut 6:4-5). Wait a minute, and then go sit near your partner(s), make eye contact and read the verses again in a softer voice. How do the two experiences differ? How does this illustrate the difference between the God who is far away and the God who is with us?

5. Commit yourself to trying one or more of the suggested tools for practicing God's presence for one month. Keep a log of

your thoughts, feelings and experiences during this period. What changes do you see happening? If possible, do this with a friend or two and compare notes.

CHAPTER 4: BEING PRESENT IN OUR BODIES

1. In your experience with Christianity, what kind of theology have you seen most often—"escape the body," "ignore the body" or "flourish in the body"? How has it affected your own view of the body in relation to your spiritual life?

2. "The Word became flesh and made his dwelling among us" (Jn 1:14). Explain in your own words the importance of this verse for our salvation.

3. Among the four biblical narratives discussed—creation, incarnation, resurrection and ascension—what is an idea you find particularly striking? Is it hard to believe? Does it fill you with wonder? Does it challenge you in some way? Spend some time talking with God about it. Listen for what he might be calling you to do, and commit yourself to acting in obedience.

4. Think about how our culture views people's bodies. Then think about Paul's statement that our bodies are temples of the Holy Spirit. How might Paul's theology retrain you in how you think about the body? What difference will it make in your life to think of your body as God's temple?

5. Odds are there are parts of your body you don't like. Maybe you don't care for your body because it isn't shaped right or it's sick or broken down. What would it mean to view your body, your *whole* body, as a perfect sacrifice to God? How might that change your view of your body?

6. What is one God-dishonoring way you have been using the parts of your body? What do you need to do to honor God with your body?

CHAPTER 5: BEING PRESENT WITH ONE ANOTHER

1. Describe relational consumerism. How much do you think you approach relationships like a relational consumer, treating people like products? What are some benefits you want from the people in your life—for example, happiness, peace, power, physical gratification, popularity?

2. Describe relational engineering. What are some of the ways we act like engineers, using people like parts to perform a function? How much do you think you approach relationships like an engineer?

3. How much relational consumerism and engineering do you see go on around you? What are some of the effects?

4. Read Isaiah 9:6-7 a couple of times slowly. *Givenness* is a humble and passive word. How does Jesus' givenness relate to the power and might described in those verses? Now read Philippians 2:5-11. What is the relationship between humility and power? How might our practice of givenness open up ways for God to bless us?

5. Where is the most challenging place for you to surrender to being given and why?

6. Identify your prominent social circles—your family, circle of friends, church, workplace, school and so on. What effect do you think it might have for you to make it a habit to practice givenness in those circles? How do you plan to approach those social circles differently today?

CHAPTER 6: THE POWER OF SURRENDER

1. In what ways do you see us playing out the question "Who will be the boss of me?"

2. Think back over the events of the last twenty-four hours. Where were you the boss of yourself without even thinking about it? Where did you surrender yourself and let God be the boss? How can you do less of the former and more of the latter?

3. What is one situation in your life that you feel some hesitation about surrendering to God? Maybe you fear that God might not give you what you feel you need. Maybe you think he will mess things up. Maybe you just don't want to surrender this issue. What is the issue? Think about the reason why you don't want to surrender it to God. What can you do to be a little more free on that issue? Whom might you need to involve for help?

4. Read slowly through the song in Philippians 2:6-11. How would you describe the self-emptying of Christ Jesus? How does his self-emptying connect with other things the song says about him?

5. What is *kenosis* and why is it important in one's spiritual life? Why do you think it is talked about relatively rarely when we discuss the Christian life?

6. Why is it important for love to be the motive for self-emptying? How might self-emptying go wrong if love isn't the motive?

7. Of the benefits of surrendering our lives and all our circumstances to God (being able to hear God's voice, becoming more intimate with him, etc.), which do you desire the most and why?

CHAPTER 7: THE POWER OF HUMILITY

1. In what ways can protecting ourselves from the world show up as a drive for personal independence? How might that evolve into protecting ourselves from God?

2. What observation about pride and humility from the story of the lost sons stood out to you?

3. What are Jesus' two giant leaps downward, and what do they teach about the character of God?

4. Describe self-emptying and humility in your own words. How are the two different? How are they complementary? How do they enter into the story of the incarnation?

5. Of the six paths into humility—truth, receptivity, selflessness, submission, servanthood and prayer—which two are you currently strongest in, and which two do you need to work on the most? Take a minute to give thanks to God for the former, and prayerfully make some concrete plans to address the latter.

6. Imagine if a church or a household were run on the basis of one key Bible verse: "God opposes the proud but shows favor to the humble" (Jas 4:6; 1 Pet 5:5). What would the life of that church or household be like?

CHAPTER 8: THE POWER OF THE SPIRIT

1. Do you think of yourself as someone who has a personal history with the Holy Spirit? What difference does it make to see yourself that way?

2. Think of a person you know who is not a Christian. In what ways do you see that God has been working in his or her history? (If you don't know, ask the person questions about his

or her life. Listen to the stories with an eye toward the presence and work of God.) How might you be able to bear witness to the presence of the Spirit in that person's life?

3. To what extent have you thought of Jesus as someone who had a personal history with the Holy Spirit? What difference does it make to see him that way?

4. Of the chapters of Jesus' personal history with the Holy Spirit related above, which one do you find most engaging and why?

5. What do you think about the Wait-Receive-Go pattern? How can you implement it in your life? If it doesn't look like Pentecost, what might it look like?

6. Review the three signs of Pentecost (wind, fire and languages). What do they mean in the Acts story, in the church today and in your life?

CHAPTER 9: PEACE: *THE WAY THAT TRANSFORMS*

1. Many American Christians are feeling restless about having more meaning in their lives. To what extent does this characterize you?

2. Talk about a situation where things are broken and people are suffering. What would you like to see happen there? How is your hope a longing for shalom?

3. Explain what compassion is and how Jesus acted it out through his life, ministry, death and resurrection. Do the same for mercy and justice.

4. Between compassion, mercy and justice, where do you feel you are strongest? Where do you feel you have the most growing to do?

Appendix 2

KEY BIBLICAL PASSAGES AND CREEDS

Who do you say I am?

MARK 8:29

This appendix is a resource intended to strengthen your grasp of the incarnation of God's Son. The incarnation is one of the key doctrines of Christianity. No other religion has a doctrine quite like it. Unfortunately, many Christians would have a hard time explaining it to a friend. I hope the following pages help you understand and form a theology of incarnation that flows within the historical stream of orthodox Christian thought.

My theology of the incarnation lies within the historical stream of orthodox Christian thought.

This appendix lays out two primary sources for the theology of the incarnation—key biblical passages about the incarnation and the major creeds of the church. The biblical passages show us how the early Christian leaders thought about who Jesus was and why God became human. The creeds let us see how the next generations of Christian leaders built a more detailed theology of the incarnation on the foundation of the Scriptures.

KEY BIBLICAL PASSAGES

Those who would become the New Testament writers were not predisposed to think of the man Jesus as being God in human skin. In fact, in the beginning it was the furthest thing from their minds. And yet the New Testament writers' views changed because of the weight of their collective personal experiences of Jesus during his life, death, resurrection and ongoing presence through the Holy Spirit. A great place to see how this process began is the Gospel of Mark. Mark has no overt references to the incarnation, but the disciples witness miraculous event after miraculous event, and eventually they are asking, "Who is this? Even the wind and the waves obey him!" (Mk 4:41).

Later Jesus would press the point, asking his disciples outright, "Who do you say I am?" (Mk 8:29). This was a burning question for Jesus' disciples. Through their search of the Scriptures and personal experiences, the early followers of Jesus became clarion voices proclaiming that in Jesus, God had become one of us and offered us new life. "Who do you say I am?" was the central issue of the early church. And it is the life-and-death question for us today. Jesus asks us in this moment, "Who do you say I am?" Following are a dozen key biblical passages you can read and meditate on as you seek to answer this question within your own heart.

Isaiah 7:14
Therefore the Lord himself will give you a sign: The virgin will conceive and give birth to a son, and will call him Immanuel.

Isaiah 9:6
For to us a child is born,
     to us a son is given,
     and the government will be on his shoulders.

And he will be called
> Wonderful Counselor, Mighty God,
> Everlasting Father, Prince of Peace. (Is 9:6)

Matthew 1:22-23

All this took place to fulfill what the Lord had said through
the prophet: "The virgin will conceive and give birth to a
son, and they will call him Immanuel" (which means "God
with us").

*(Note: In the following passage, "Word" refers to God the Son,
the second person of the Trinity.)*

John 1:1-18

In the beginning was the Word, and the Word was with God,
and the Word was God. He was with God in the beginning.
Through him all things were made; without him nothing
was made that has been made. In him was life, and that life
was the light of all mankind. The light shines in the darkness,
and the darkness has not overcome it.

There was a man sent from God whose name was John. He
came as a witness to testify concerning that light, so that
through him all might believe. He himself was not the light;
he came only as a witness to the light.

The true light that gives light to everyone was coming
into the world. He was in the world, and though the world
was made through him, the world did not recognize him. He
came to that which was his own, but his own did not receive
him. Yet to all who did receive him, to those who believed
in his name, he gave the right to become children of God —
children born not of natural descent, nor of human decision
or a husband's will, but born of God.

The Word became flesh and made his dwelling among us. We have seen his glory, the glory of the one and only Son, who came from the Father, full of grace and truth.

(John testified concerning him. He cried out, saying, "This is the one I spoke about when I said, 'He who comes after me has surpassed me because he was before me.'") Out of his fullness we have all received grace in place of grace already given. For the law was given through Moses; grace and truth came through Jesus Christ. No one has ever seen God, but the one and only Son, who is himself God and is in closest relationship with the Father, has made him known.

Philippians 2:6-11
In your relationships with one another, have the same mindset as Christ Jesus:

Who, being in very nature God,
    did not consider equality with God something to be
      used to his own advantage;
rather, he made himself nothing
    by taking the very nature of a servant,
    being made in human likeness.
And being found in appearance as a man,
    he humbled himself
    by becoming obedient to death—
    even death on a cross!

    Therefore God exalted him to the highest place
      and gave him the name that is above every name,
    that at the name of Jesus every knee should bow,
      in heaven and on earth and under the earth,
    and every tongue acknowledge that Jesus Christ is Lord,
      to the glory of God the Father.

Colossians 1:15-20

The Son is the image of the invisible God, the firstborn over all creation. For in him all things were created: things in heaven and on earth, visible and invisible, whether thrones or powers or rulers or authorities; all things have been created through him and for him. He is before all things, and in him all things hold together. And he is the head of the body, the church; he is the beginning and the firstborn from among the dead, so that in everything he might have the supremacy. For God was pleased to have all his fullness dwell in him, and through him to reconcile to himself all things, whether things on earth or things in heaven, by making peace through his blood, shed on the cross.

Hebrews 1:3-4

The Son is the radiance of God's glory and the exact representation of his being, sustaining all things by his powerful word. After he had provided purification for sins, he sat down at the right hand of the Majesty in heaven. So he became as much superior to the angels as the name he has inherited is superior to theirs.

Hebrews 2:5-9

It is not to angels that he has subjected the world to come, about which we are speaking. But there is a place where someone has testified:

"What is mankind that you are mindful of them,
    a son of man that you care for him?
You made them a little lower than the angels;
    you crowned them with glory and honor
    and put everything under their feet."

In putting everything under them, God left nothing that is not subject to them. Yet at present we do not see everything subject to them. But we do see Jesus, who was made lower than the angels for a little while, now crowned with glory and honor because he suffered death, so that by the grace of God he might taste death for everyone.

Hebrews 2:14-18

Since the children have flesh and blood, he too shared in their humanity so that by his death he might break the power of him who holds the power of death—that is, the devil—and free those who all their lives were held in slavery by their fear of death. For surely it is not angels he helps, but Abraham's descendants. For this reason he had to be made like them, fully human in every way, in order that he might become a merciful and faithful high priest in service to God, and that he might make atonement for the sins of the people. Because he himself suffered when he was tempted, he is able to help those who are being tempted.

Hebrews 10:5-7

Therefore, when Christ came into the world, he said:

"Sacrifice and offering you did not desire,
    but a body you prepared for me;
with burnt offerings and sin offerings
    you were not pleased.
Then I said, 'Here I am—it is written about me in the
        scroll—
    I have come to do your will, my God.'"

1 John 4:2-3

This is how you can recognize the Spirit of God: Every spirit that acknowledges that Jesus Christ has come in the flesh is from God, but every spirit that does not acknowledge Jesus is not from God. This is the spirit of the antichrist, which you have heard is coming and even now is already in the world.

1 John 4:7-12
Dear friends, let us love one another, for love comes from God. Everyone who loves has been born of God and knows God. Whoever does not love does not know God, because God is love. This is how God showed his love among us: He sent his one and only Son into the world that we might live through him. This is love: not that we loved God, but that he loved us and sent his Son as an atoning sacrifice for our sins. Dear friends, since God so loved us, we also ought to love one another. No one has ever seen God; but if we love one another, God lives in us and his love is made complete in us.

MAJOR CHRISTIAN CREEDS

Besides Scripture, the other main light that has guided the church through the centuries has been the ecumenical creeds. *Ecumenical* in this case means "universal." These are theological formulas that sum up the teaching of Scripture and state it in a way that is considered to be "necessary for salvation, or at least good for the well-being of the Christian Church."[1] The ecumenical creeds were established before the church split between an eastern branch (Eastern Orthodoxy) and a western branch (Roman Catholicism). They represent the voice of the unified church, and for this reason Christians have viewed the ecumenical creeds as having great authority. The ecumenical creeds underscore two key points about God:

The Trinity: There is one God who exists in three persons, Father, Son and Holy Spirit.

The incarnation: Jesus is God the Son who became human.

The Apostles' Creed, Nicene Creed and Chalcedonian Creed are especially interested to clarify the outlines of the incarnation and its role in God's plan of salvation. As you read them, you might notice how the theology of who Jesus is develops more detail. This process took some four hundred years and was driven by the church's desire for theological refinement and clarity in worship, and also by the need to settle questions that arose through various theological controversies during this time.

These creeds frame orthodox Christian theology, but they have been subjected to rigorous questioning. Controversies have arisen about both the Trinity and the incarnation. Rather than engage those complex discussions, I present the creeds here in the spirit of the early church, in which nonscriptural documents were regularly used during worship for the purpose of building up the community of believers. Throughout this book you will notice that the theology of the incarnation I put forth is built on Scripture and the ecumenical creeds.

Apostles' Creed (third/fourth century)

I believe in God, the Father Almighty,
   creator of heaven and earth.

I believe in Jesus Christ, his only Son, our Lord.
   He was conceived by the power of the Holy Spirit
   and born of the Virgin Mary.
   He suffered under Pontius Pilate,
   was crucified, dead, and was buried.

He descended to the dead.
On the third day he rose again.
He ascended into heaven,
and is seated at the right hand of the Father.
He will come again to judge the living and the dead.

I believe in the Holy Spirit,
the holy catholic Church,
the communion of saints,
the forgiveness of sins,
the resurrection of the body,
and the Life everlasting. Amen.[2]

Nicene Creed (325 C.E.)

We believe in one God,
the Father, the Almighty,
maker of heaven and earth,
of all that is, seen and unseen.

We believe in one Lord, Jesus Christ,
the only Son of God,
eternally begotten of the Father,
God from God, Light from Light,
true God from true God,
begotten, not made,
of one Being with the Father;
through him all things were made.
For us and for our salvation
he came down from heaven,
was incarnate of the Holy Spirit and the Virgin Mary
and became truly human.
For our sake he was crucified under Pontius Pilate;

he suffered death and was buried.
On the third day he rose again
in accordance with the Scriptures;
he ascended into heaven
and is seated at the right hand of the Father.
He will come again in glory to judge the living and the
    dead,
and his kingdom will have no end.

We believe in the Holy Spirit, the Lord, the giver of life,
    who proceeds from the Father and the Son,
    who with the Father and the Son is worshiped and
        glorified,
    who has spoken through the prophets.
    We believe in one holy catholic and apostolic Church.
    We acknowledge one baptism for the forgiveness of sins.
    We look for the resurrection of the dead,
    and the life of the world to come. Amen.[3]

Chalcedonian Creed (451 C.E.)

We, then, following the holy Fathers, all with one consent, teach men to confess one and the same Son, our Lord Jesus Christ, the same perfect in Godhead and also perfect in manhood; truly God and truly man, of a reasonable soul and body; consubstantial with us according to the manhood; in all things like unto us, without sin; begotten before all ages of the Father according to the Godhead, and in these latter days, for us and for our salvation, born of the virgin Mary, the mother of God, according to the manhood; one and the same Christ, Son, Lord, Only-begotten, to be acknowledged in two natures, inconfusedly, unchangeably, indivisibly, inseparably; the distinction of natures being by no means taken away by the union, but rather the property of each nature being preserved, and concurring in one Person and one Subsistence, not parted or divided into two persons, but one and the same Son, and only begotten, God the Word, the Lord Jesus Christ, as the prophets from the beginning have declared concerning him, and the Lord Jesus Christ himself taught us, and the Creed of the holy Fathers has handed down to us.[4]

Prayer Exercise
Worshiping Jesus

Choose a section of either the Scriptures or the ecumenical creeds. As you slowly read, stop at whatever point you are struck by something. You might be drawn by a particular word or phrase, or you might feel yourself wanting to pull away. Pay attention to your response to the text, and make the movements of your heart the subject of your prayer. Talk openly and honestly to God about who Jesus is and what God has done.

If you have faith to believe that in Jesus, God really did become human and save us, worship him and don't hold back!

NOTES

INTRODUCTION

[1]"Continuous partial attention" is a term that was coined by author Linda Stone in 1998.

CHAPTER 1: Shining Like Stars

[1]Brian Kolodiejchuk, ed. and commentator, *Mother Teresa, Come Be My Light* (New York: Doubleday, 2007), p. 44.

[2]Malcolm Muggeridge, *Something Beautiful for God: Mother Teresa of Calcutta* (New York: Harper & Row, 1971), p. 17.

[3]Ibid., p. 127.

[4]Paul may have had the book of Daniel in mind when he compared us to shining stars. In Daniel 12:3, the angel Michael tells Daniel that in the end times "those who are wise will shine like the brightness of the heavens, and those who lead many to righteousness, like the stars forever and ever."

CHAPTER 2: Purpose

[1]In the Synoptic Gospels (Matthew, Mark and Luke), Jesus does not describe himself as "the one sent by God" very often. See Matthew 15:24; Mark 9:37; Luke 4:43; 9:48; 10:16. In those Gospels, Jesus refers to himself with other titles such as "Son of Man." When we look through the lens of the incarnation, "sent by God" points to the centrality of mission, and "Son of Man" asserts Jesus' solidarity with humanity.

[2]Christopher Wright, *The Mission of God* (Downers Grove, IL: InterVarsity, 2006), p. 212.

[3]Cornelius Plantinga, *Not the Way It's Supposed to Be: A Breviary of Sin* (Grand Rapids: Eerdmans, 1995), p. 10.

[4]John 3:17; 3:34; 4:34; 5:23; 5:24; 5:30; 5:36; 5:37; 5:38; 6:29; 6:38; 6:39; 6:44; 6:57; 7:16; 7:18; 7:28; 7:29; 7:33; 8:16; 8:18; 8:26; 8:29; 8:42; 9:4; 10:36; 11:42;

12:44; 12:45; 12:49; 13:16; 13:20; 14:24; 15:21; 16:5; 17:3; 17:8; 17:18; 17:21; 17:23; 17:25; 18:24; 20:21.

CHAPTER 3: BEING PRESENT WITH GOD

[1] Brother Lawrence, *The Practice of the Presence of God* (Grand Rapids: Spire, 1967), p. 15.

[2] Ibid., p. 13.

[3] Ibid.

[4] John N. Oswalt, *The NIV Application Commentary: Isaiah* (Grand Rapids: Zondervan, 2003), p. 142.

[5] Leon Morris, *The Gospel According to Matthew* (Grand Rapids: Eerdmans, 1992), p. 125.

[6] See Parker Palmer, *Let Your Life Speak* (San Francisco: Jossey-Bass, 2000).

[7] Craig Groeschel, *The Christian Atheist* (Grand Rapids: Zondervan, 2010), p. 13.

[8] Quoted by Rick Duvall, "Are You Suffering from Information Overload?" Relationship Economy website, July 14, 2009, www.relationship-economy .com/?p=5222.

[9] See Mac Slocum, "Don't Blame the Information for Your Bad Habits," *O'Reilly Radar*, November 29, 2011, http://radar.oreilly.com/2011/11/ information-overload-overconsumption-diet.html.

[10] Richard Foster, *Prayer: Finding the Heart's True Home* (San Francisco: Harper, 1992), p. 1.

[11] Frank Laubach, *Letters by a Modern Mystic* (Colorado Springs: Purposeful Design, 2007), entry for March 9, 1930.

[12] Foster, *Prayer*, p. 126.

[13] Ibid., p. 127.

[14] Ibid., p. 119.

CHAPTER 4: Being Present in Our Bodies

[1] Rodney Clapp, *Tortured Wonders* (Grand Rapids: Brazos, 2004), p. 34.

[2] Gerrit Dawson, *Jesus Ascended: The Meaning of Christ's Continuing Incarnation* (New York: T & T Clark, 2001), p. 189.

[3] Clapp, *Tortured Wonders*, pp. 47-48.

[4] See William Casey, *A Guide to Living in the Truth: St. Benedict's Teaching on Humility* (Ligouri, MO: Ligouri/Triumph, 2001).

[5] Dallas Willard, *Renovation of the Heart* (Colorado Springs: NavPress, 2002), p. 160.

CHAPTER 5: Being Present with One Another

[1]Louise Story, "Anywhere the Eye Can See, It's Likely to See an Ad," *New York Times*, January 15, 2007.

CHAPTER 6: The Power of Surrender

[1]Donald Macleod, *The Person of Christ* (Downers Grove, IL: InterVarsity Press, 1998), p. 213.

[2]Richard Foster, *Prayer: Finding the Heart's True Home* (San Francisco: Harper, 1992), p. 52.

[3]Ibid., p. 54.

[4]Thomas Dubay, *Fire Within* (San Francisco: Ignatius, 1989), p. 131.

[5]David G. Benner, *Surrender to Love* (Downers Grove, IL: InterVarsity Press, 2003), p. 60.

[6]Brian Kolodiejchuk, ed. and commentator, *Mother Teresa, Where There Is Love, There Is God* (New York: Doubleday, 2010), p. 12.

[7]Margaret Silf, *Inner Compass* (Chicago: Loyola Press, 1999), p. 158.

[8]Greg L. Hawkins and Cally Parkinson, *Move: What 1,000 Churches Reveal About Spiritual Growth* (Grand Rapids: Zondervan, 2011), p. 84.

[9]Gerald May, *Addiction and Grace* (New York: HarperOne, 1988).

[10]Foster, *Prayer*, pp. 49-50.

CHAPTER 7: The Power of Humility

[1]Henri Nouwen, *The Return of the Prodigal Son* (New York: Doubleday, 1992), p. 71.

[2]Henri Nouwen, *The Selfless Way of Christ: Downward Mobility and the Spiritual Life* (Maryknoll, NY: Orbis, 2007).

[3]Ibid., pp. 38-39.

[4]Ibid., p. 83.

[5]William Casey, *A Guide to Living in the Truth: St. Benedict's Teaching on Humility* (Ligouri, MO: Ligouri/Triumph, 2001), p. 56.

[6]John Cassian, *The Twelve Books of the Institutes of the Coenobia*, trans. Edgar C. S. Gibson, second series, vol. 11 of Nicene and Post-Nicene Fathers (Peabody, MA: Hendrickson, 1995), chaps. I-VII.

[7]Nouwen, *Selfless Way of Christ*, p. 26.

[8]Casey, *Guide to Living in the Truth*, p. 1.

CHAPTER 8: The Power of the Spirit

[1]Gerald E. Hawthorne, *The Presence and the Power* (Dallas: Word, 1991), p. 182.

[2]Klaus Issler, "Jesus' Example: Prototype of the Dependent, Spirit-Filled Life," in *Jesus in Trinitarian Perspective*, ed. Fred Sanders and Klaus Issler, (Nashville: B & H, 2007), p. 191.

[3]Jack Hayford, *Spirit-Filled: The Overflowing Power of the Holy Spirit* (Wheaton, IL: Tyndale, 1984), p. 13.

[4]Thomas Dubay, *Fire Within* (San Francisco: Ignatius, 1989), p. 141.

CHAPTER 9: Peace

[1]Gary Haugen, *Just Courage* (Downers Grove, IL: InterVarsity Press, 2008), p. 17.

[2]Walter Brueggemann, *Living Toward a Vision: Biblical Reflections on Shalom* (New York: United Church Press, 1982), p. 15.

[3]Cornelius Plantinga, *Not the Way It's Supposed to Be: A Breviary of Sin* (Grand Rapids: Eerdmans, 1995), p. 10.

[4]Gregory of Nyssa, quoted in Donald Macleod, *The Person of Christ* (Downers Grove, IL: InterVarsity Press, 1998), p. 160.

[5]Haugen, *Just Courage*, 92.

[6]Philip Yancey, *What's So Amazing About Grace?* (Grand Rapids: Zondervan, 1997), p. 16.

[7]Haugen, *Just Courage*, p. 47.

CONCLUSION

[1]See James Tabor, *Blind Descent* (New York: Random House, 2010).

[2]Quoted in Shane Claiborne, Jonathan Wilson-Hartgrove and Enuma Okoro, *Common Prayer: A Liturgy for Ordinary Radicals* (Grand Rapids: Zondervan, 2010), p. 209.

[3]Malcom Muggeridge, *Something Beautiful for God: Mother Teresa of Calcutta* (New York: Harper & Row, 1971), p. 31.

[4]Ibid., p. 126.

[5]Ibid., p. 17.

[6]Brian Kolodiejchuck, ed., *Mother Teresa: Where There Is Love, There Is God* (New York: Doubleday, 2010), p. 359.

APPENDIX 2

[1]Philip Schaff, *The Creeds of Christendom* (Grand Rapids: Baker, 1990), 1:4.

[2]Book of Common Prayer.

[3]1988 Ecumenical Version.

[4]Text quoted from Schaff, *Creeds of Christendom*, 2:62.